Cambridge Elements

Elements in Shakespeare and Pedagogy
edited by
Liam E. Semler
The University of Sydney
Gillian Woods
University of Oxford

TRANSDISCIPLINARY SHAKESPEARE PEDAGOGY

Coen Heijes
University of Groningen

Shaftesbury Road, Cambridge CB2 8EA, United Kingdom

One Liberty Plaza, 20th Floor, New York, NY 10006, USA

477 Williamstown Road, Port Melbourne, VIC 3207, Australia

314–321, 3rd Floor, Plot 3, Splendor Forum, Jasola District Centre,
New Delhi – 110025, India

103 Penang Road, #05–06/07, Visioncrest Commercial, Singapore 238467

Cambridge University Press is part of Cambridge University Press & Assessment,
a department of the University of Cambridge.

We share the University's mission to contribute to society through the pursuit
of education, learning and research at the highest international levels of excellence.

www.cambridge.org
Information on this title: www.cambridge.org/9781009564298

DOI: 10.1017/9781009564267

© Coen Heijes 2025

This publication is in copyright. Subject to statutory exception and to the provisions
of relevant collective licensing agreements, no reproduction of any part may take place
without the written permission of Cambridge University Press & Assessment.

When citing this work, please include a reference to the DOI 10.1017/9781009564267

First published 2025

A catalogue record for this publication is available from the British Library

ISBN 978-1-009-56429-8 Paperback
ISSN 2632-816X (online)
ISSN 2632-8151 (print)

Cambridge University Press & Assessment has no responsibility for the persistence
or accuracy of URLs for external or third-party internet websites referred to in this
publication and does not guarantee that any content on such websites is, or will
remain, accurate or appropriate.

Transdisciplinary Shakespeare Pedagogy

Elements in Shakespeare and Pedagogy

DOI: 10.1017/9781009564267
First published online: February 2025

Coen Heijes
University of Groningen

Author for correspondence: Coen Heijes, c.p.a.heijes@rug.nl

ABSTRACT: Building on a general trend in academia towards convergence in teaching and research, in which interdisciplinarity and relevance are cornerstones, *Transdisciplinary Shakespeare Pedagogy* offers a sense both of the opportunities and of the challenges in teaching Shakespeare beyond the confines of the English literature department by setting up structural partnerships across disciplinary units and provides possible ways forward on the road to wider cooperation, collaboration and integration between curriculums, teachers and students of different disciplines. With Shakespeare studies increasingly under fire, the author analyses, through four recent case studies of university courses for a variety of students, the potential for integration of Shakespeare studies, social sciences and societal challenges.

KEYWORDS: Shakespeare, pedagogy, transdisciplinary, interdisciplinary, education

© Coen Heijes 2025

ISBNs: 9781009564298 (PB), 9781009564267 (OC)
ISSNs: 2632-816X (online), 2632-8151 (print)

Contents

1 Introduction   1

2 Initial Steps: Shakespeare and Management   15

3 Widening the Terrain: Shakespeare, Leadership and Twenty-First-Century Challenges   32

4 Transdisciplinary Teaching: Shakespeare, Social Justice and Collaboration   51

5 Crossing Borders: International Transdisciplinarity   69

6 Conclusion   86

References   92

1 Introduction

During the 'Teaching Shakespeare' seminar of the British Shakespeare Association conference in 2021 one of the participants, Abhishek Sarkar, warned in his paper on teaching Shakespeare in Bengal that it would be 'eminently possible that Shakespeare in the following decades will be confined to a select minority of especially committed academics' (Sarkar, 2021). Concerns such as these are not new at Shakespeare conferences. At the '(In)Significant Shakespeare' seminars, which David Ruiter and I organised in 2021 (World Shakespeare Congress, Singapore) and 2022 (Shakespeare Association of America, Jacksonville) and also at the 'Shakespeare, Here, Now: Locating Relevance in Early Modern Drama' seminar (British Shakespeare Association, Liverpool 2023), which I participated in, similar sentiments were expressed by those present. Nor are these concerns new or even restricted to Shakespeare studies. In the preface to the updated edition of Nussbaum's book on the role of the humanities in education the 'first thing to be said is that they [the humanities] are clearly in trouble all over the world' and five years after her first edition, Nussbaum's rallying cry has been translated in over twenty languages (Nussbaum, 2017: xiii). The arts and humanities, and with them Shakespeare studies, are increasingly under fire and have to demonstrate their significance to avoid further budget cuts. Traditional arguments about Shakespeare providing a moral infrastructure which cannot be translated into mere economic profitability, about Shakespeare's enduring universality and the infinite variety of human characters in his plays, or about the challenging and ever-changing perspectives that his work offers seem not to cut the ice anymore in these discussions.

Responses to both the internal and the external calls for significance are varied. Virtually all Shakespeare conferences and symposiums, whether in Singapore, Stratford-upon-Avon, Townsville, Seoul, Liverpool, Jacksonville, the Cape Winelands, Budapest or online have of late aimed at connecting Shakespeare studies with the broader challenges of present-day society and many of its burning issues, such as migration, racism, xenophobia, populism, poverty, and moral, social and ecological sustainability, with keynote speakers arguing that the time of sitting on the fence is over. Theatre productions, special issues, articles and books likewise aim at demonstrating the deep and intricate entanglement between Shakespeare and social justice (e.g. Ruiter, 2020; Thurman & Young, 2023; the Bloomsbury 'Shakespeare and Social Justice' series). In education too, there is a move from a traditional, historically contextualised and text-oriented perspective towards a more action-oriented approach in which social awareness and justice figure prominently, and culturally relevant and anti-racist, feminist and decolonising pedagogies gain ground (e.g. Bickley & Stevens, 2023; Dadabhoy & Mehdizadeh, 2023; Eklund & Hyman, 2019; Karim-Cooper, 2021; Panjwani, 2022; Semler, Hansen & Manuel, 2023; Smith, 2021; Thompson & Turchi, 2016). In addition, Shakespeare is being increasingly applied outside its immediate literary and theatrical circle as a tool to help people recover or develop specific skills, as among inmates, persons who suffer from PTSD or other mental health issues, persons with learning disabilities or even managers to help hone their leadership skills (e.g. Bates, 2013; Cavanagh & Rowland, 2023; Johanson, 2023; Mackenzie, 2023; Stavreva, 2022).

In engaging with many of these topics, we, as Shakespeareans, inevitably and knowingly enter the terrain of other disciplines. The 2021 British Shakespeare Association conference explicitly asked for 'new interdisciplinary approaches in order to develop innovative ways of performing, writing about, and teaching Shakespeare' (British, 2021). Dadabhoy and Mehdizadeh argue that 'literary studies, and Shakespeare studies more specifically, can learn from other disciplines such as sociology, cultural studies, and education' (2023: 11). Likewise, it may also work the other way around and Shakespeare courses focused on today's societal challenges may prove a valuable addition for students outside the English department. This general move towards interdisciplinarity and relevance raises inevitable challenges for Shakespeare studies. One may wonder to what extent Shakespeare scholars are qualified to teach about topics that are not their immediate specialisation. In *Anti-Racist Shakespeare*, Dadabhoy and Mehdizadeh indicate how Shakespeare or English literature teachers may feel limited by a lack of expertise and admit that they are 'asking instructors to be race scholars as well as Shakespeare scholars' (2023: 33). Moving Shakespeare into any of #MeToo, #BLM, #Autocracy or #CultureWars debates is entering a terrain that instructors in the social sciences have explored in far more detail. At the same time, even though our forays into other disciplines are increasingly being advocated and discussed in academia, the reality of collaborative teaching projects across disciplines in universities is scarce, as I will discuss in more detail in Section 1.1. While we have started engaging with social sciences in research and teaching, most of our teaching is still limited to students of Shakespeare or literature within the traditional English department or to students from other faculties taking courses in the English department. The amount of cooperation, let alone collaboration, between Shakespeare teachers and those in the social sciences departments is few and far between and in this Element I aim to move beyond these barriers and demonstrate, by way of four recent case studies, how teaching Shakespeare may also take place outside the English department and result in structural partnerships across departmental borders. The four case studies give a sense not only of the opportunities but also of the hurdles, on a personal, a pedagogical and an institutional level, in teaching Shakespeare beyond the English literature department, and provide possible ways forward on the road to transdisciplinary Shakespeare pedagogy.

The developments in moving across disciplines do not stand on their own, but fit a wider pattern in academic institutions towards convergence in research and teaching. Two elements are of specific importance in this educational approach: (1) The approach is driven by specific, current societal problems and aims at examining and addressing these and thereby enhancing society; (2) convergence education works across and integrates multiple disciplines, recognising that one needs several perspectives, disciplines, methodologies and forms of expertise to address these challenges. While originally the approach more focused on science, technology, engineering and mathematics (the so-called STEM group), convergence education and research has started to include disciplines within the social sciences and humanities as well. Some authors have argued for including the arts (with a capital A) explicitly in the STEM group and advocated calling it the STEAM group instead (Harris & Wynn, 2012; Guyotte et al., 2014; Robinson, 2017). Likewise, authors have argued how convergence research in the social sciences can, for example, be of use in addressing and mitigating institutional racism. In their research on addressing structural racism and its implications for health inequity, Neely et al. have spanned disciplines including education, epidemiology, social work, sociology, and urban planning in order to 'facilitate and encourage future transdisciplinary collaboration to dismantle structural racism and disrupt its role in shaping health inequity' (2020: 381). The term 'transdisciplinary' that is used in the previous citation is one that is increasingly applied. Although definitions of transdisciplinarity still vary among scholars, there is general consensus on the inclusion of at least two specific aspects: (1) the focus of the research and the teaching is on real-life problems in the world around us and (2) the research and teaching transcends and integrates disciplinary paradigms (Bernstein, 2015; Crowe et al., 2013; Flavian, 2024; Interagency, 2022; Leavy, 2011; Pedersen, 2016).

Transdisciplinarity can perhaps best be understood as part of the following continuum: disciplinarity – multidisciplinarity – interdisciplinarity – transdisciplinarity. Disciplinarity exists within the context of one specific discipline, sharing basic assumptions and methodologies; the stronger these (institutionalised) boundaries, the further specialisations tend to develop within one's discipline. Multidisciplinary approaches tend to involve two or more disciplines, each of which brings their own knowledge to bear without specifically aiming to integrate concepts or methodologies. Interdisciplinarity involves learning from and integrating knowledge of several different disciplines, knitting them more closely together in a process to deepen understanding or improve skills. Without wanting to discredit the benefits of disciplinary teaching, both interdisciplinary and multidisciplinary approaches have stimulated disciplines in cooperating and collaborating and contributed to exposing the limitations of taking a disciplinary approach. A transdisciplinary approach goes a step further on the continuum as it transcends disciplines in that it is fundamentally problem-oriented rather than discipline-driven. Building on and transgressing several disciplinary boundaries it responds to real-life problem-based questions and requires disciplinary crossing to help students in addressing complex political, social and environmental problems. The social justice–oriented perspective is an important element in transdisciplinarity and Leavy argues that there 'is a moral imperative driving the need for transdisciplinary approaches to real-world issues of import' (Leavy, 2011: 50). The borders between the aforementioned approaches are, however, far from clear-cut and the pedagogy in Dadabhoy and Mehdizadeh's *Anti-Racist Shakespeare* (2023), which the authors define as interdisciplinary, might equally be qualified as transdisciplinary, considering the important 'emancipatory aims' (32) underlying the publication. In this Element, the four case studies are dealing with transdisciplinary teaching and structural bridging across disciplinary boundaries within universities, a topic which earlier research on Shakespeare pedagogy has rarely touched upon. Next we consider recent calls for and research on collaboration across boundaries within Shakespeare studies, and in particular as related to teaching and indicate in more detail what seems to be lacking and to what extent this Element addresses these gaps.

1.1 Crossing Boundaries, Teaching Shakespeare

In crossing boundaries, one of the first questions to be asked is, 'why Shakespeare?' Should we use a White hegemonic icon with a contested history, tainted by accusations of both cultural supremacy and a limited, Anglocentric perspective? And more to the point, should we use this supposedly timeless, universal icon in addressing social (in)justice? It is a question that Shakespeare teachers have to address these days and they do so in a variety of ways as exemplified in the collection of essays on teaching social justice and Shakespeare (Eklund & Hyman, 2019). Desai was inspired by James Baldwin's essay 'Why I Stopped Hating Shakespeare' (Baldwin, 1964) and argues how reading Shakespeare can 'promote imaginative experimentation and collaboration' (Desai, 2019: 34). Jones describes how the wide availability of Shakespeare productions and adaptations, such as in MIT's Global Shakespeare archive stimulates students to move away from a 'timeless universal icon [... and] value a multiplicity of timely, locally active Shakespeares' (Jones, 2019: 62). Using Shakespeare in this way helped her students to overcome a tendency not to draw too much attention to themselves and instead engage more actively and openly on topics of social justice, Jones argues. Osborne draws attention to the perilous state that the arts and humanities are in due to a decline in funding and a general scepticism about their economic value, particularly in rural parts of the United States. He argues how Shakespeare has the power to enrich students and prompt them to suspend and question their own values, also drawing on his own personal experiences as a student: '[M]any of the students I teach are, like I was, economically underprivileged first-generation students for whom university-level humanities study provides one of first among already few opportunities for self-transformation' (Osborne, 2019: 107). Della Gatta presents an argument for the usefulness of Shakespeare in a timeframe where disinformation, alternative facts and fake news have resulted in a questioning and manipulation of truth. She argues how teaching Shakespearean plots and language may serve as a 'platform for learning to distinguish between fact and fiction [. . . and] discussing how characters know what they know' (Della Gatta, 2019: 169).

Teaching Shakespeare in connection with social justice is not always an easy process, as is borne out, for example, by Demeter, who describes how his class on antiracist Shakespeare and African-American literature worked counterproductively as it only seemed to reinforce 'Shakespeare's position at the top of a cultural, curricular, and ideological hierarchy, while framing oppositional responses thereto as impotent rejoinders' (Demeter, 2019: 74). Even here, though, the author argues that this does not mean that Shakespeare cannot be used to address antiracism, but rather that we cannot simply rely on juxtaposing oppositional perspectives. In a similar vein, Kemp argues how the Globe's comparison of cross-dressing characters in *Twelfth Night* to the experiences of transgender and gender nonconforming youth (Tosh, 2017) is not helpful for his students as it 'places undue emphasis on the garment and thus problematically blurs trans identity with the language of disguise' (Kemp, 2019: 40). Like Demeter, Kemp does not discredit the use of Shakespeare, but argues for lectures which shift away from the interior/exterior divide and focus instead on using Shakespeare characters that experience homelessness or sexual violence, which he argues are much closer to transgender experiences. As teachers of Shakespeare and social justice, we have to choose our battles and our strategies wisely.

In the recent volume *Reimagining Shakespeare Education* (Semler, Hansen & Manuel, 2023), the editors added as its subtitle 'Teaching and Learning through Collaboration', which runs as a red thread through the publication which explores collaborative projects in five different settings: schools, universities, the public, digitisation and performance. A second red thread in the volume coincides with the movement towards aligning Shakespeare with social justice, exploring topics such as identity, diversity and community, all the while (critically) highlighting the potential rewards of Shakespeare education. In summarising these collaborative projects, the editors indicate how they are often 'prominences of energy arcing out from creative hotspots within institutional or organisational bases [... which] exemplify creative yearnings to reach out, rethink, reframe, do more, do different and do better' (Semler, Hansen & Manuel, 2023: 5). The crossing of disciplinary boundaries is one of the elements that the volume aims to address, although the editors simultaneously warn of the dangers of these specific, creative projects being stifled by funding and viability as institutional Shakespeare education is always in danger of routinisation and managerialism (Semler, Hansen & Manuel, 2023: 10).

The separate section on 'reimagining Shakespeare with/in universities' consists of four collaborative projects and each 'challenges and productively responds to boundaries – physical, geographical, institutional or socioeconomic – to enable pedagogical innovation in tertiary Shakespeare education' (Semler, Hansen & Manuel, 2023: 87). These projects include a collaboration between the University of Birmingham and the Royal Shakespeare Company in an effort to 'dismantle binaries between teaching, research and theatre practice' (Davies, 2023: 100) and another, more institutionalised, collaborative project between Shakespeare's Globe and King's College London who have offered a joint Shakespeare Studies Master's degree programme (Karim-Cooper et al., 2023). A third collaborative project took place across physical boundaries in a cooperation between the University of Warwick, United Kingdom, and Monash University in Australia. The authors argued how the geographical distance and the experimentation with the possibilities of technology to work across this generated not only a sense of fun, but also an awareness of differences in culture, knowledge and societal priorities as '"Local and Global Shakespeares" fostered a collaborative ethos and a uniquely affective and playful form of intercultural competence' (Gregory, García Ochoa & Prescott, 2023: 126). The final chapter of the section on university education brings together two groups of students who write and respond to each other's essays: students of the course 'Shakespeare in Text and Performance' at Emory University in Atlanta, Georgia, and prison students of the class 'Shakespeare and Me', by Shakespeare Central, some of whom have extensive educational backgrounds, while others do not. Through this form of collaboration between very divergent groups, the teachers argue that students will not only understand the plays better but also learn more about themselves as 'they can draw direct parallels from their own lives to the complex predicaments and hard decisions faced by Shakespeare's people' (Cavanagh & Rowland, 2023: 137).

All of these collaborative projects in the university section are without a doubt impressive and they exemplify the challenges and potential benefits of crossing boundaries between countries, between universities and between universities and other institutions such as prisons and theatre companies. What seems to be lacking, though, is a more detailed analysis of crossing boundaries across disciplines and faculties within universities. To a large extent, we still consider these crossings from the perspective of Shakespeare studies, English literature or at best the humanities in general. Nor is this seeming lack of attention uncommon in other publications and case studies on Shakespeare, social justice and collaboration. Eklund and Hyman, in their introduction to *Teaching Social Justice Through Shakespeare*, indicate the necessity for crossing over to new fields of study, for engaging with 'the demands of the current moment [...] and] for early modern studies to undertake a new kind of engaged truth-seeking and truth-making' (Eklund & Hyman, 2019: 5). There is a strong awareness of the necessity to 'encourage students to make connections between the classroom and the world beyond it – and to examine their assumptions about a range of social, racial, economic, and environmental issues and the people they affect' (Eklund & Hyman, 2019: 10). The essays in the volume are timely, inspiring and of immense value to teachers and students in connecting the variety of the many worlds of local Shakespeares to social justice (and injustice) and providing a classroom where students engage in active discussions and action in many different contexts. As such, they fully align with the editors' belief that they contribute to a cultural shift 'that sees that "time's up" for instrumental, exclusionary approaches to higher education, and which reimagines early modern texts as potentially fundamental to collaborative meaning-making and liberatory action' (Eklund & Hyman, 2019: 20). At the same time, this volume too is largely limited to the English literature classroom, excluding cohorts of students who might also benefit from the approaches in this volume and offers scant evidence of collaborating with and teaching at other faculties and disciplines, with the large majority of contributors working at departments of English studies. The most recently edited publication on Shakespeare and education at the time of writing (Bickley & Stevens, 2023) differs from the aforementioned in that it also provides a historical perspective, although more than half of the contributions are focused on the twenty-first century and the editors state that 'perhaps one of the timeliest questions to emerge from the sequence of essays is how and how far Shakespeare should play an active role in promoting social equality, inclusiveness and justice' (Bickley & Stevens, 2023: 2). Responding to the threat to the arts and humanities in a neoliberal world, the editors argue how the 'writers in this collection testify to the vibrant potentiality of Shakespearean pedagogy', which includes another series of impressive and creative essays on teaching Shakespeare in conjunction with topics such as anti-racism, xenophobia, identity, transgender struggles and ecological challenges (Hahn, 2023; Hansen, 2023; Hennessey, 2023; Turchi, 2023). Once again, however, the reaching out does not include teaching across faculties and disciplines, and although the editors mention that 'the authors are by no means all university based (as is often the case with edited volumes)', the large majority is based in or related to the English departments (Bickley & Stevens, 2023: 1).

A specific branch of the social justice interest focuses itself not so much on a specific topic, such as sexism, gender identity or racism, but rather covers the theme of leadership as such, which they argue lies at the root of many of these problems. Within this sphere, there are two main approaches. On the one hand, there is a focus on political leadership, often connected to leaders who employ a populist, xenophobic and autocratic leadership style. Sometimes, these leaders are referred to directly, such as Donald Trump (Mentz, 2019; Wilson, 2020); sometimes they are only implied (Greenblatt, 2018). This approach often tends to include a personal element in the form of a strong sense of disagreement with these political leaders. On the other hand, there is a focus on managerial leaders, where the main idea generally is trying to teach or improve leadership skills. Of all the areas where Shakespeare is being taught across disciplines, this is the area which has attracted most attention, with MBAs and business schools using Shakespeare's 'status' to tempt prospective students. In the next section (case study one) I explore this in more detail.

While I have argued that the main stream of research and teaching on Shakespeare and social justice and its calls for collaboration and venturing beyond the traditional English literature classrooms seems to exclude reaching out to students in other departments and disciplines, I do not mean to imply that students from other disciplines do not take English units. There is a fair amount of student mobility across units of study and at many English departments, including at our own university, non-English major students take literature courses. However, what seems to be lacking are explicit, thoughtfully built, structural partnerships across disciplinary units, even though several case studies in volumes on Shakespeare and pedagogy might well be suitable for such a venture. An interesting example is Hobgood's description of a class she taught in Japan on Shakespeare and disability studies. The class coincided with the mass killing of nineteen residents of a care centre for people with mental and physical disabilities by an employee who seemingly acted 'out of mercy' (Hobgood, 2019: 46). The combination of students lacking a general familiarity with Shakespeare, a societal stigma in Japan surrounding mental disability and the recent, horrible events led Hobgood to approach *Macbeth* through accessible adaptations such as the Manga Shakespeare series (Appignanesi, 2008) and the OMG Shakespeare series (Carbone, 2016) and the screening of *Throne of Blood* (Kurosawa, 1957). In this way, through the intermediary of insanity in *Macbeth*, the class provided a space for creating a dialogue about disability, which might not have been possible if the topic had been approached head on. Classes such as these employ Shakespeare to ultimately discuss relevant topics and Hobgood's own multidisciplinary background, in English, Teaching and Women's Studies, might help explain the potential which classes like these would have, not only for connecting with students of other disciplines, but also for crossing the boundaries between disciplinary departments. Somewhat comparable is a course that Kirsten Mendoza taught at Vanderbilt University 'that fulfilled a requirements for arts and sciences undergraduates' (Mendoza, 2019: 102). Kirsten Mendoza is an assistant professor of English and Human Rights, and in this particular class none of her students were English majors; most were in fact hesitant rather than enthusiastic about reading Shakespeare. At the time of the course, two former football players of the university had been convicted of aggravated rape of an unconscious female student, which Mendoza wanted to incorporate in her lectures. The combination of studying and discussing *The Rape of Lucrece*, the recent rape trial and the topic of sexual assault helped students 'navigate the psychosomatic terrain of engaging with known systemic violence' (Mendoza, 2019: 103).

What these two, impressive, classes share is the use of Shakespeare with a student cohort relatively unfamiliar with Shakespeare by teachers willing to cross disciplines in order to address very relevant and controversial topics in an effective manner. Although the breeching of disciplines as such was never the intent of these courses nor do these essays pay specific attention to it, they do provide powerful examples of how Shakespeare can be taught beyond the traditional English literature segment and setting up transdisciplinary courses across disciplinary boundaries. This is something that I will build on and explore in more detail in this Element, as it addresses a relevant but relatively unexplored area in Shakespeare and pedagogy: Why, if Shakespeare has so much to offer and provides such a useful platform, why, if the humanities and Shakespeare studies are under fire and have to defend their usefulness, why, if student numbers are dropping in Shakespeare studies, why, if we more and more engage with social justice and therewith also enter the domain of social sciences, why, if transdisciplinarity is increasingly important in teaching and research, why, then, do we mostly limit ourselves at universities to the English literature classrooms in the English departments, even in cutting-edge volumes on Shakespeare and teaching? It would be presumptuous to pretend to answer all of these questions, but I do hope that my own experiences in venturing beyond the (classroom in the) English department would offer the reader some ideas and tools regarding both the possibilities and the challenges that this form of transdisciplinary teaching may offer to both teachers and students. At the risk of repeating myself, I would like to stress that this is not about pulling in students from other cohorts to follow an English minor or elective. Instead, I am explicitly talking about structural bridging across disciplines within university contexts via institutionally built curriculums, a hitherto underdeveloped area within Shakespeare pedagogy. Breaking through these institutional walls can be difficult and in this Element I focus therefor not only on the content and teaching methods of these courses, but also on the process of crossing these departmental boundaries and the pitfalls, challenges, and (sometimes necessary) compromises that one is confronted with. Next, I briefly discuss the methodology used and the structure of the Element.

1.2 Method and Structure

As is often the case in research on Shakespeare and pedagogy (e.g. Bickley & Stevens, 2023; Dadabhoy & Mehdizadeh, 2023; Eklund & Hyman, 2019; Semler, Hansen & Manuel, 2023; Thompson & Turchi, 2016), the research is (partly) grounded in case studies in which the researchers themselves participated. The use of case studies is a powerful strategy in a situation where observation, detailed description, complexity and contextuality are important aspects of the research and is particularly useful in exploratory research. The case studies that form the basis of this Element consist of four different courses which I have developed and (co-)taught from 2018 to 2023. Characteristic for case study research is the use of multiple sources of evidence (triangulation), which helps to increase the validity of the research (Flick, 2019; Hennink, Hutter & Bailey, 2020; Yin, 2018). In this Element I employ methodological triangulation by using a variety of methodological tools: literature review and document study, participant observation and interviews. Literature review and document study focused on previous studies on Shakespeare and pedagogy and Shakespeare and social justice and on more specific, course-related documents, such as course descriptions, exercises, student products and assessments, course evaluations. Participant observation took place during lectures, assessment sessions and also included discussions with students, co-teachers, course convenors, programme coordinators, programme directors, deans and other staff outside lectures during which the researcher was present. An important aspect is to ensure the privacy of students involved in the research, so that they are not placed in an undesirable position, even if it is only a request to participate in future research, which is why all references to individual students have been anonymised. Interviews took place after lectures and focused on the evaluation and content of the course. In most case studies on pedagogy and Shakespeare, the researcher is part of the case studies and interacts with the students, which means that the researcher has to be alert in avoiding selective perception. My own background is multidisciplinary, both academically (MAs in English Language and Literature; Cultural Studies (specialisation diversity studies); Shakespeare Studies; Shakespeare & Theatre; Business Studies and a PhD in Culture and Communication) and professionally (an interviewer; an advisor diversity policy for profit and non-profit organisations; an English teacher at secondary school; a manager and trainer in the Netherlands, the Caribbean and Eastern Europe; and an assistant professor and fellow at the University of Groningen). Even though a diversity in background might be of help in understanding and appreciating different perspectives during the research, one always has to be aware of one's own subjectivity. In this Element, I have aimed at further doing so by employing member check (allowing coteachers to read relevant passages and where necessary discuss adjustments). Likewise, peer debriefing was a useful tool: the interpretations of the researcher were evaluated by colleagues in the field, in this case the general editors of the series *Shakespeare and Pedagogy* and the readers of the draft version, all of whom generously provided invaluable comments.

The four case studies are discussed respectively in Sections 2–5, after which Section 6 rounds off with a conclusion. The order of the four case studies is chronological: the first course started in 2018, the second course in 2019, the third course started in 2021 and the last one in 2022. All courses reached out to students beyond the English literature cohort and attention points in the process towards transdisciplinarity which I discuss in these sections include:

- how would I convince course and programme coordinators of the necessity of the courses;
- which compromises would I have to make;
- which student groups would I aim for – this would imply which faculties to choose, which year-levels the students would need to have, which

nationalities, which prerequisite knowledge (Shakespeare and/or social sciences);
- which relevant present-day topics would I focus on;
- which Shakespeare plays, productions or adaptations would be most helpful;
- which teaching methods would I apply;
- which products would I want the students to deliver and how would I evaluate these;
- would I be teaching by myself or would I include other teachers as well;
- how would I evaluate the course;
- how would I address the potential lack of Shakespeare knowledge among the students;
- and how would I balance appreciating the beauty of Shakespeare's words with the more prosaic, but ever so relevant topics which social sciences address?

The general throughline in this Element is that the courses have become increasingly complex and challenging, moving from case study one to case study four, in part also because I increasingly gained more experience myself. This development is reflected in the changes in all of the aforementioned more specific throughlines moving from the first course to the last. In Section 2 I discuss monodisciplinary groups of mainly Dutch students from the Faculty of Economics and Business at the University of Groningen centred around well-defined, individual student products (the writing of bachelor and master's theses). The course in Section 3 is taught at the University College Groningen and includes students with a variety of disciplines and national backgrounds and end products that are group-based. In Section 4 I discuss a course taught at the Honours College Groningen, which takes place over a period of two years and includes a variety of other teachers and also a visit to the United Kingdom. The final course, in Section 5, is an international cooperation between the University of Groningen and the University of Nottingham Trent, where students of English literature cooperate online in groups with students from other disciplines around the topic of the Other and present and discuss these final products online as well.

2 Initial Steps: Shakespeare and Management

Faculty: Economics and Business, University of Groningen.

My first steps towards transdisciplinary teaching involving Shakespeare started in 2018 and took place at the Faculty of Economics and Business, University of Groningen. The faculty has, as its name already implies, two main themes: one is more macro-oriented and focuses on the economy as a whole, mainly employing large-scale databases and quantitative research methods; the other (in which the course was situated) is more micro-oriented, focusing on (groups of) individuals or companies, while discussing topics such as human resources, leadership, international business, accounting and control. At the time, my teaching was largely involved with culture, communication and leadership, particularly as related to gender and racial and ethnic studies, both within and across national borders. My research, on the other hand, had by now moved away from this field and focused squarely on Shakespeare, presentism and performance. As these two strands (my teaching and my research) had not yet come satisfactorily together, I decided to embark on a course which would intertwine the two and I chose the bachelor and master's thesis courses for management students as a starting-point to integrate leadership studies with Shakespeare. This first case study reflects challenges, errors, misunderstandings, uncertainties, but also enthusiasm, success and inspiration. I suppose if one were to compare this case study with a piece of music, something like Debussy's prelude *Des Pas sur La Neige* (Footsteps in the Snow) would sound just about right: tentative, dissonant notes, striving for harmony, achieving glimmers of hope, but never quite finding a perfect resolution. Which perhaps makes sense for the first steps on the journey towards transdisciplinary teaching.

There were several reasons to start with these specific courses. First, they met my main criterion which was to integrate social sciences topics with the study of Shakespeare and reach out to students who would not normally engage with Shakespeare. As this was challenging enough, I decided to start relatively safe and simple. Rather than opting for a complex and diverse group of students, I chose a more uniform, monodisciplinary group of students at one specific faculty. In addition, I did not want to have to invent a course from scratch, but preferred a course that had a predetermined structure and end-products for students, while simultaneously allowing an amount of freedom in the choice of topics. Bachelor and master's thesis supervision, where students are allowed to choose from a list of potential topics which are determined by the expertise of the specific supervisor, seemed to fit these requirements. Students have to list three topics, ranked in order of preference, after which they are assigned, as far as possible, to their preferred choice. Also the amount of students was manageable, as bachelor supervision usually encompassed eight or ten (Dutch) students simultaneously, while master's thesis supervision was generally on an individual basis, with no more than four students at the same time. Also, in the past, I had already taught several bachelor and master's thesis courses at the faculty, although they had generally focused on the impact of cross-cultural perception and communication in relation to diversity studies, usually involving gender, race or ethnicity. What also helped was a burgeoning and growing awareness at the time within the faculty that crossing disciplines might be necessary for the development of the field in addressing the increasingly complex, societal and organisational challenges (Faculty, 2016, 2021).

Finally, a decent amount of research had already been done by others on the topic of Shakespeare, leadership and management as part of a broader interest in the relation between canonical literature and management. As already briefly mentioned in the previous section, research on leadership and Shakespeare had focused on both political and managerial leadership and the latter one would be particularly useful for bachelor and master's students in the proposed course. In the twenty-first century, management literature expressed a tentative, but slowly growing interest in canonical literature as a source for leadership studies and education. In particular, leadership studies that focused on aspects such as power relations, ethics and justice, emotions such as jealousy, doubt and fear, or more generally the 'softer' and ambiguous sides of leadership, turned to canonical literature to help aspiring leaders gain different perspectives on the challenges and the emotional cost of leadership. (e.g. Ciulla, 2019; Deckers, 2021; Egan, 2000; Etzold, 2012; Olivier, 2013; Pujante & Gregor, 2023; Stein, 2005; Warner, 2007). Within this field of research, Shakespeare is the author whom researchers turned to most, in particular building on his history plays and tragedies to help analyse leadership challenges and dilemmas. While this type of research is still in its infancy and demonstrates some shortcomings, such as a tendency to use anecdotal evidence or a failure to properly connect leadership literature with Shakespeare studies, the amount of previous research would provide students of the bachelor and master's course with a framework to build upon.

Having determined what I wanted, the next step was contacting the current course coordinators, neither of whom I knew, with my proposal and I did feel some trepidation. While my proposal fit the trend towards interdisciplinarity, within the Faculty of Economics and Business this trend was mainly limited to reaching across the several departments within the faculty or, at best, to other social sciences faculties. Crossing over towards the humanities, let alone Shakespeare, for a bachelor or master's thesis, had never been done before at the Faculty of Economics and Business in Groningen. Also, the course description of the bachelor thesis read, for example, that the 'knowledge, capabilities and research methods as achieved in the bachelor programme should be considered the starting point for this course' (Bachelor's, 2018). This conflicted, at least in part, with what I had in mind for my proposed bachelor and master's thesis courses. My concerns were justified, but only in part: the bachelor thesis coordinator was immediately sold and accepted the proposal without any hesitation; the master's thesis coordinator, however, was of two minds about the proposal. She mentioned how she, as a student, would have loved to have had a thesis topic such as the one I proposed available when she was doing her master's in management. However, at the same time she was not entirely convinced that the current generation of students would be interested in a topic that seemed to be so far off the beaten track. She also advised me that any thesis would have to pass the normal hurdle of the second assessors (not involved in teaching), who might be quite critical in their decision whether the thesis would be well enough on-topic in order to warrant a pass. It took some serious discussion, but in the end, we agreed that I would be allowed to put my proposal to the students, provided I would frame the course description in a more enticing manner, while simultaneously warning them of the challenges the topic might encompass. It resulted in the following, abbreviated, course description for the master's thesis.

2.1 Course Description for Students: Master's Thesis

> ### Cross-Disciplinary Approaches to Management and Control
>
> Over the last decades, the management and control literature has gradually sought more cross-disciplinary and innovative approaches in addressing the challenges that managers face. While business studies as such are a relatively new discipline, humanities have been studying leadership and management for over 2,000 years. It is, however, not until recently that academics and managers, as well as renowned business schools, have been exploring ways of drawing on the richness of history, philosophy, and literature from a variety of cultures to shed light on these challenges that managers face. Incentives and motivation, ethics, leadership, diversity, trust, sustainability, and personnel and cultural controls are some of the areas that are seeing increasing use of other disciplines to complement traditional approaches to management and control.
>
> In this master's thesis, you will build on this approach and zoom in specifically on the managerial usefulness of arguably the best known, as well as the best-selling author of all times, William Shakespeare. No fictional writer has been appropriated, or misappropriated, more by business schools than this playwright (both on account of his popularity and based on the infinite variety and ambivalence that permeates his works), to study management and control issues from a different perspective.
>
> No prior knowledge of the play(s) or the author is required: we are not a Shakespeare class, and citations from the playwright may be used in present-day translations, which are available online. As we are embarking on a relatively unexplored area of cross-disciplinary research, this research theme group might be of specific interest to students who are not afraid to think out of the box. Particularly, an inquisitive and creative mind, the ability to cope with ambivalence and work relatively independently, and a drive to explore innovative and complex approaches to management

(cont.)

(studies) are requisites that will prove to be useful and stimulating for prospective participants of this group.

Hours per week	Variable
Number of weeks	18–24
Teaching method	Group sessions & individual supervision
Assessment	Bachelor thesis, master's thesis
Course type	Bachelor & master
Student composition	Monodisciplinary (social sciences, specialisation management); Dutch students (bachelor thesis), international (master's thesis)
Number of instructors	1
ECTS	10 (BA thesis), 20 (MA thesis)

Learning Outcomes and Output

The bachelor's and master's theses respectively conclude the bachelor and master programmes at the University of Groningen. Both courses aim at testing the student's academic capabilities. In the bachelor setting, students 'have to show that they are able to think in an academic way, perform specific delineated research in the field of Business and Management, and report this study accordingly' (Bachelor's, 2018). The purpose of the master's thesis is that the students demonstrate their ability to do research independently within a chosen specialisation. The learning objectives for the master's thesis require a student to be 'able to:

1. Recognise and analyse a problem in the specialist field;
2. Do a literature search on a certain theme within the specialist field;
3. Make a research design of a complex problem in the specialist field and employ specific research methods;

> (cont.)
> 4. Collect qualitative or quantitative data using appropriate data collection methods, analyse data and/or to design a solution in the specialist field;
> 5. Draw conclusions, make recommendations, generalise findings and identify limitations of the research in the specialist field;
> 6. Write a (research) report in a systematic manner by exhibiting a clear and precise use of English.' (Master's, 2019)

The bachelor thesis has a maximum word count of 6,500, and the master's thesis has a preferred maximum of 12,000 words (excluding references and appendices).

2.2 Course Set-Up and Lectures

Having jumped through all the required hoops, it all looked fine enough on paper, but as I was soon about to discover, the proof of the pudding is in the eating and my first venture into reaching out to students beyond the traditional English literature cohort would be a greater challenge than I had anticipated. No matter how well I thought I had prepared, no matter the nod of approval from the course coordinators, no matter my own enthusiasm and no matter the relatively homogeneous groups or the standardised structure of the courses, reality was about to start rearing its complex and unpredictable head. As detailed earlier, and in response to the coordinator's suggestion, I had left the course description for both the bachelor and the master's thesis group on purpose relatively broad, to allow the students freedom to determine which specific topics would be of most interest to them, but also to draw in an adequate amount of students. Perhaps not unexpectedly, I received several requests from bachelor and master's students for further clarification, as exemplified by this email:

> I am considering choosing the bachelor thesis course *A cross-disciplinary approach to leadership, management and control*. Now, I don't as yet understand the Shakespeare idea. I don't quite understand what it is that we, in choosing a research

> topic, need to do with this. Are we expected to write the entire research from his 'perspective'?
> For me it is, as I think you will notice, all still fairly unclear. I hope you will be able to supply me with some further clarifying information as regards the theme of the thesis and the influence of Shakespeare.
> I look forward to hearing from you!

In my reply to this (bachelor) student I pointed out the option to analyse leadership, ethics or cross-cultural cooperation through Shakespeare's plays, but, disappointingly, my answer was not satisfactory as the student did not enrol in the course. In hindsight, my reply was vague and merely repetitive of the course description as such, partly caused by my own lack of experience in this new approach to teaching Shakespeare across disciplines. In the end, however, ten students enrolled in the bachelor thesis, six of whom had it as their first choice, three as their second choice and one as their third choice. For the master's thesis four students enrolled, all of them first choice and the maximum number allowed for supervision. Notwithstanding the vagueness of the course description, this was quite a satisfactory result and I was set up for my first venture into transdisciplinary Shakespeare with a group of students not studying English literature.

The first lecture for both groups was on the one hand explanatory, as most students had no real idea of what they were getting into and were waiting for me to tell them what it was that they were going to (have to) do or what options they had. For me, the opening lecture also offered a first opportunity to get a basic idea of why the students had chosen this topic, what their knowledge of Shakespeare was, where their interests lay, and also to what extent they already had an idea about the topics they wanted to address. During the first session of the bachelor thesis, for which I had asked the students beforehand to email me their reasons for choosing this specific bachelor theme, it became clear that most students knew next to nothing about Shakespeare. Their main reasons for choosing this course varied between a desire to challenge themselves, a more general interest in literature and a wish to tread outside the traditional approach towards management:

> I was the nurse in our school production of Romeo and Juliet, but I really don't remember anything about it. I guess, I wanted to do something different now, after all these years of management books.

In the master's thesis group, composed of students from the Netherlands, Germany and Mexico, similar sentiments were expressed, the difference being that they were expressed more strongly and all students had a keen interest in canonical literature, as exemplified in the words of this student:

> A theme that utilizes arts and humanities for a Business Administration MSc programme can be seen as quite unconventional, and many people were surprised when they heard that I was going to be focusing on canonical literature for my study. However, it was the uniqueness of the theme that lured me into making it my first theme choice. I have also been interested in canonical literature for some time, but could never find much time and energy to read it, due to the amount of time I have to spend on my (interesting, but more conventional) studies. [This theme is] allowing me to combine my passions for this research.

Following the explanatory phase, we engaged in a more exploratory discussion, as some bachelor students (and all master's students) already had some rather general and embryonic ideas, which we discussed and explored further, while simultaneously we explored more in general possible topics and plays that might prove to be useful for students. By way of example I discussed *Henry V* with the bachelor students, being the play most studied in research on Shakespeare and management. This orientation phase took relatively long, mainly because they were not used to make meaningful cross-overs between disciplines and Shakespeare was relatively unknown to these students.

In order to address these points, I first asked students to explore why the humanities in general might be relevant for management research and also to find previous research on this topic. Building on that, we would focus on Shakespeare and get a sense of the extent to which his plays had been (ab)used in research or teaching on Shakespeare and management before and how their thesis might build on this and potentially explore new areas. At the end of this phase, all students had managed to choose a suitable topic and research question. This first phase of moving towards research questions took more time than usual, mainly because students had to enter hitherto unfamiliar disciplines. Within the bachelor thesis, one of the students opted for a literature review analysing the current state of research regarding Shakespeare and leadership and providing recommendations for further research. Two other students compared specific models of leadership (Morden, 1997; Winston & Patterson, 2006) to Shakespeare's presentation of leaders. The other students chose more theme-oriented approaches and explored topics including morale and leadership, motivation, ethical leadership, transformational leadership, persuasion and rhetoric. In drawing parallels and indicating contrasts between management literature and Shakespeare plays (in particular *Henry V*, *Julius Caesar*, *Richard III* and *Antony and Cleopatra*), the students aimed at revealing potential blind spots in management literature.

For the master's thesis too, the first scheduled session was unlike 'regular' thesis supervision sessions I had had before and was mainly spent answering questions, providing tentative suggestions, and to a large extent brainstorming. Normally, these first master's thesis sessions would be on an individual basis, but considering the new territory for all four students, I had decided on a group session. I had scheduled twice forty-five minutes with a fifteen-minute break for this session, but in the end we took two and a half hours without a break, due largely to their enthusiasm for the topic and their love of literature. From the start, the eagerness to cooperate, to learn from and help each other was prevalent and all other sessions from then on were also group-based. Even the final session in which students defend their thesis in the presence of the second assessor (which is traditionally on an individual basis) would be a group session at the specific request of the students. There was a strong sense of 'we started this together and we will finish it together'. Rarely have I seen a group of students so supportive as this group, critically reading and commenting on all of each other's drafts for each session, no doubt in part caused by a sense of being able to explore a shared passion for literature within the constraints of their chosen master in management studies.

In their final thesis all students expressed in their preface thanks to their group members, as illustrated by phrases such as the 'sharp and startling feedback' or the 'comments, support and advice, [which] helped me break through many obstacles'. While two of these students stuck to Shakespeare in their master's thesis, two others ventured further afield. One student chose to draw a comparison between Shakespeare and two other authors in the thesis, based on the following two research questions:

> Are Machiavelli, Shakespeare and Sun Tzu used for similar or different themes and perspectives in the leadership literature and why is this?
>
> What are the main benefits and limitations of using these writings in leadership studies?

The fourth student had asked me whether it needed to include Shakespeare or if another author would also be allowed, to which I had replied in the positive, not wanting to rein in their enthusiasm or deter them in a topic and field of research which was enough of a challenge as it was. It resulted, surprisingly, in a master's thesis which interrogated how fairy tales we grow up with reflect and challenge cultural differences in leadership in three different cultural clusters: the Anglo, the Germanic Europe and the Confucian Asia Cluster (House et al., 2004). In hindsight, I probably would not allow such a diversion again, but in this hard-working and supportive group it worked.

The next major hurdle during this course was of a methodological nature. Methodology is an important part in any research involving social sciences (and is regularly underdeveloped or taken for granted in Shakespeare studies). As social sciences studies not only employs quantitative but also more qualitative research methods, the students were well versed in systematic literature review.

Preceding the start of the bachelor and master's thesis at the faculty, all students are required to take the 5 ECTS course Academic Skills. This includes not only traditional academic conventions such as structure, argumentation, developing a research question, using peer-reviewed academic literature, citations and references, but also focuses on the use of the various methodological tools that are available for research purposes. Both quantitative and qualitative tools are studied, including the use of surveys, questionnaires and regression analysis, interview techniques and the analysis of interviews, (participant) observation and literature review. However, their knowledge of content or narrative analysis, which is what they would also have to apply in studying Shakespeare texts and determining their relevance, was limited and we addressed that during a separate session on methodology. Most students used a combination of literature review and content and narrative analysis, while the master's students combined this with more advanced analytical tools of identifying and coding key concepts about themes or arguments in the text.

After this relatively slow start, the lectures followed a traditional pattern whereby we had periodic sessions, for which students prepared part of their thesis, which we discussed in group sessions, with students learning from and discussing each other's progress. These next phases would include a systematic literature review which would first focus on the existing literature on a specific social sciences topic, after which they would confront these findings with a specific play (or plays) of Shakespeare and use content analysis to determine where the twain did meet, where they diverged, which lacunas existed and what might be learned from this. After bringing these two strands together in their findings, they would engage in a discussion, indicate the limitations of their thesis and provide suggestions for further research. While the theses showed a wide variety in the themes they addressed, all students demonstrated how analysing a Shakespearean text complemented gaps in existing leadership research on, in the words of a student, 'topics such as emotions and the fluidity, moral questionability, and the fluid socially constructed nature of leadership'. Many argued (rightly) that this field of research was still in its infancy and a common and not entirely unexpected suggestion to address this was their recommendation 'to use interdisciplinary research teams', something that still happens few and far between in Shakespeare or in leadership research. Some bachelor students went a step further and suggested in their limitations and further research section that future cooperation between students of these different disciplines might also be beneficial:

> A final limitation of this research is that this research is conducted by a business student. Therefore there was no prior knowledge of canonical literature and the work of Shakespeare. More knowledge about canonical literature could lead to new insights and maybe a deeper interpretation of the text. [...A] research conducted by a business student and a student canonical literature might be interesting, as suggested in the limitations, because this could lead to new insights, given that both students are knowledgeable of their own disciplines.

This form of cooperation between students of different disciplines was something which would gain traction in the next two case studies (Sections 3 and 4) and led in the final and most recent case study (Section 5) to a direct cooperation between students of English literature and social sciences students. Next I discuss the aftermath of the bachelor and master's thesis courses, the grading, course evaluations, compromises and what I learned from those in more detail.

2.3 Aftermath
2.3.1 Grading

In the end, one bachelor student dropped out halfway through the course, due to personal reasons not related to the course itself. The remaining students all finished their bachelor and master's thesis within the allotted timeframe. In grading the theses, a standard protocol is used including grading by the supervisor and an independent second assessor (not involved in the teaching). If no consensus is reached about the grade, a third assessor considers the thesis and makes a decision which needs to be approved by the general coordinator of the thesis programme. While I considered all submitted theses to be of sufficient quality, I have to admit I was slightly worried about any second assessor's evaluation, as I was pretty much operating in uncharted territory. I worked with a total of four different second assessors, two of whom had some experience in crossing disciplines (one on the topic of management and cultural industries, one on management and happiness) and another two who were strictly monodisciplinary. None of the second assessors had any experience with crossing boundaries between English literature, let alone Shakespeare, and management studies. One may understand my nervousness, also in light of the previously mentioned warning by the master's thesis coordinator. The grading was based on standardised forms of the Faculty of Economics & Business comprising scores on seventeen different aspects. The three main categories are scientific quality (70 per cent of the grade, including problem analysis, research question, methodology, use of literature, data collection, data description, conclusion, interpretation of findings and limitations, implications and recommendations), process (20 per cent: degree of independence, use of feedback, professional attitude) and report (10 per cent: structure, data presentation, language, referencing, abstract).

Even though I had gone through all the necessary hoops to get the thesis proposals accepted at the faculty, and even though I thought the students had done well enough to quite well, I expected some stiff discussion with the second assessors about grading. These grading sessions between supervisor and second assessor are intended to be a professional discussion where one listens respectfully to one another's arguments. However, I found myself in a different mind-set, coming to the sessions fully armed and prepared to defend the work of my students. I need not have bothered. All four of the second assessors expressed an enthusiasm about the originality of the theses, the courage of the students to take on an innovative approach to management studies and the findings and discussions that this resulted in. All students passed in one go, none of the second assessors' grades were lower than mine and in fact most of the grades they gave were actually higher than my own. To my surprise, the second assessor for the master's thesis, a business controller and a hardcore accounting professor of many years with a plethora of international publications wanted to upgrade all four proposed grades by one point, considering them to be good to very good. His argumentation was on the one hand built on the daring and innovative approach to accounting and control, which he thought merited publication in social sciences journals, and on the other hand he argued that the theses zoomed in precisely on those elements of accounting and control where traditional handbooks and research often faltered. Seemingly I had unconsciously graded the theses lower than they merited, possibly caused by a lingering uncertainty whether the topic of the theses would be relevant enough for monodisciplinary management students.

2.3.2 Student Evaluations

These comprise standard thesis evaluation forms, which are written by individual students after the course. They are sent directly to the administrative staff and are next (anonymised) communicated to the teacher after the grading process has been finalised. The students grade five different categories: (1) In general, I am satisfied with supervision; (2) my supervisor supervised me professionally; (3) my supervisor took sufficient time to answer my questions; (4) my supervisor provided me with useful feedback; (5) my supervisor provided me with feedback within the ten working days' term. The maximum grade they can give is a five and the average of the five grades is the 'overall' grade for the course. For the bachelor theses, the overall grade was a 4.6, for the master's thesis the overall grade was a 5.0. Although I had expected good results, I had not expected the evaluation grades to be so high, also considering the various obstacles both students and I had had to face during the course.

While grades are of importance to the coordinators of the thesis programmes, for me as a teacher the more qualitative comments, which students may include, are always more useful as they point out in more detail what went well, what would need improvement and potential blind spots in the course. Bachelor students highly appreciated the structure, the feedback sessions, the 'cross-disciplinary approach', the 'fun' and 'the atmosphere in which it took place', resulting in a high overall score:

> Dr. Heijes completely livened up the subject for me, provided quality feedback (on time), supported the entire group in a very professional manner. Honestly after hearing some bad stories about other supervisors I was very surprised at the extremely high quality of supervision of mister Heijes.

In a sense, it also comes with the territory and the choices I had made earlier. The moment I had started to ask students to engage in a type of research and a topic with which they were relatively unacquainted, I realised I would also have to put in the extra mile myself in order to help these management students navigate the challenging waters of transdisciplinary Shakespeare. Points of criticism concerned the lack of written feedback at the end, and rightly so as students had only received the grading form at the end of the course. While these included some small qualitative comments, students would have liked to have had more specific feedback: 'After all the work we put in the thesis, this was quite a disappointment.' Another point of criticism touched upon the lack of alignment between the methodology course Academic Skills and the methodology used in this bachelor thesis, which I discussed earlier and one student suggested that it 'would have been nice if the supervisor was already involved during Academic Skills'. It was the very same suggestion I had also made earlier to the coordinator, and I was pleasantly surprised to see that these suggestions were realised the year after. While the master's thesis evaluations did not include any suggestions for improvement, they did include more personal reflections on the course and the effect it had had on the students themselves, as exemplified by this student's comments:

> While doing this research and writing this paper, I found out that words are so powerful. This may be because I was not that familiar with Shakespeare when I started this research. In Shakespeare's play, Henry V inspired his soldiers to fight alongside him against France. And in the same manner Shakespeare has inspired me. One day, I might become also a leader. I am sure that I will remember this research then. [. . . .] Furthermore I would like to thank the Royal Shakespeare Company and other organizations related to Shakespeare for their efforts. I hope that you will proceed with this, in order to touch even more people, and hopefully also students like me, with the great works that Shakespeare has brought to this world.

It never ceases to amaze me, a veteran of so many years, how students who are new to Shakespeare can still be so deeply and personally affected by his plays.

2.3.3 Compromises

One of the issues that I had to address was the set-up of the courses in which I had allowed students a relatively free rein to pick subjects of their choice. Within the bachelor group it resulted in a focus on four different plays as mentioned earlier. With a group of English literature students this might perhaps not have been a problem, but with a group that was relatively new to Shakespeare it was, as it resulted in many of the students not being able to participate fully in the group discussion if another play than the one they wrote on was being discussed. As the students read and discussed each other's research, this presented a problem. In the master's thesis group, one student moved partly and another one moved completely beyond Shakespeare, focusing on fairy tales. While these were intriguing and innovative approaches, ones through which I myself also learned a lot, at the same time it required a significant effort, timewise, on my part in order to effectively supervise these students. This was something the students themselves were also keenly aware of, as expressed in the preface of a master's thesis:

> I would first like to thank my supervisor, dr. Cornelis Heijes, for allowing me to combine my passions for this research. He went above and beyond the call of duty in guiding and helping me, as other people were also often surprised (and jealous) when I told them how much genuine interest and support I received from my supervisor.

While it was rewarding to experience that my efforts were appreciated and not in vain and while personal enthusiasm and the effort of a teacher is an important driver in education, at the same time it does take time, more time than was allotted for the course. Aiming to address this, but also wanting to make the bachelor course in particular more cohesive and less a set of individual research papers, I made some changes to the set-up of the course the year after. Rather than giving them a free hand, students could now choose from a series of related and predetermined topics and themes on Shakespeare and leadership. This was a necessary compromise I had to make, which inevitably resulted in a more straitjacketed approach. At the same time, it also generated more discussion and depth amongst students during the lectures, which was the main idea behind the change. While the overall score of the bachelor thesis in the new set-up rose from 4.6 to 4.8, at the same time and perhaps not unsurprisingly one of the students mentioned in the evaluation form as point of concern: 'small range of thesis topics'.

Another compromise was a direct result of my decision to start simple, to make the course accessible to students not studying English literature and to fit the course into an existing structure within a specific student segment. This was a conscious choice, as it was my first venture into transdisciplinary teaching and I simply did not feel equipped enough to start from scratch entirely. It did mean, however, that I was not able to vary the assignments or the end-products that the students had to work on, which left less room for experimentation or for assignments and products that I felt might be more suitable. The course had to fit pre-determined requirements and I wanted more diversity and room to manoeuvre in regarding student composition, teaching methods, assignments and evaluation methods. Also, and another consequence of my initial choice for 'safe and simple', I wanted to move further afield and address not only managerial, but also other topics more aligned to social (in)justice, which would be more in line with my expertise in diversity studies.

A final compromise was the use of language, as I allowed the students to read modern-day translations of the plays, although in their final thesis they had to use quotes in the original language. This was something else I would want to change in order to provide a better balance between Shakespeare and social sciences. Finding a proper balance is always a fine line to walk when one engages in transdisciplinary teaching. For the current cohort of students, the amount of Shakespeare to which they were introduced and which they were working with was, at times, overwhelming. At the same time, most of them cherished the new approach and the insights that this provided, not only in engaging with managerial problems, but also finding actual pleasure in exploring plays (and productions) by Shakespeare which also seemed to reignite their pleasure in reading literature. However, for me, as a teacher, the course was leaning too much towards social sciences, and I was not entirely comfortable with this. While I thoroughly enjoyed the lectures and introducing non-English literature students to Shakespeare and to all the potential benefits that could be derived from connecting different disciplines, somehow I needed to find a way to address this balance, which led to the development of a new course at the University College Groningen.

3 Widening the Terrain: Shakespeare, Leadership and Twenty-First-Century Challenges

Faculty: University College Groningen (offers an interdisciplinary bachelor programme called Liberal Arts and Sciences), University of Groningen.

Having picked up a certain amount of experience with teaching transdisciplinary Shakespeare to non-English literature students and integrating this with bachelor and master's thesis courses, I decided the time was right to continue the process by aiming for a regular style lecture rather than a thesis course, which would allow for more freedom in designing the course. Also, I wanted to move beyond management students and aim for other social sciences students as well in an effort to link up with my experience in diversity studies. The course that I envisioned would ideally be one that was not boxed in, but a regular course that students could choose as an elective. While realising this would likely be more challenging and inevitably require a fair amount of energy and time on my account, the (perhaps unexpected) success at the faculty of management had given me more than enough energy to go down this path. The University College Groningen seemed like the perfect place to start: it is a faculty at the University of Groningen which offers a bachelor in liberal arts and sciences (after which students may continue to do a master at a faculty of their choice). It offers

> an academic degree with a genuinely interdisciplinary outlook, freedom of choice and a collaborative and guided approach to learning in a stimulating and globally challenging environment [... enabling] students to learn how to

> apply a creative approach in finding solutions for complex global challenges. (University, 2023)

In spite of all the obstacles and compromises I experienced in introducing students at the faculty of management to Shakespeare, I also felt a profound sense of achievement caused not only by the students' evaluations and enthusiasm or even the grading by the second assessors but also by my own joy in guiding these students towards their bachelor and master's thesis in management, based in part on Shakespeare. In my overconfidence, I naively expected other faculties, and in particular this one, to be equally interested in the potential that transdisciplinary courses encompassing Shakespeare would offer. On this basis, I made an appointment with the dean of the faculty to discuss my, in truth, as yet quite embryonic and rather vague ideas. The fact that the dean had been a professor at the faculty of management, before his current position, would also work in my favour, I reasoned. In hindsight, I suppose I had expected that mere enthusiasm might be contagious. I was wrong. We had a discussion about the benefits of transdisciplinary education and Shakespeare and while he was not averse to the idea, he was not overenthusiastic either. I had not been able to communicate my ideas coherently and convincingly (I must have sounded like the archbishop in *Henry V* trying to explain Salic law) and while my idea was deemed 'interesting', I realised that I simply had not done my homework.

Another approach was needed. I had to be more persuasive, political, almost manipulative and I decided to contact the chair of the Humanities and member of the Board of Education of the University College Groningen. This time, however, I would be prepared. I studied the current courses on offer at the faculty, I spoke to two professors who taught courses which shared some distant similarities with the type of course I had in mind and I had a close look at the specific research interests of the chair I needed to convince. In the end, I prepared three different options for possible courses which I thought might be of interest to students at the faculty. The first option was a general course titled 'Shakespeare and today's global challenges', which would 'focus on first year's students and build on Shakespeare's perennial questions about our society and the problems we face, both at the individual and the societal level'. The course would include study of (1) *The Taming of the Shrew* and gender issues, (2) *Othello* and racial discourse, (3) *Romeo and Juliet* and homophobia, (4) *The Merchant of Venice*, religious conflict and antisemitism, (5) *Richard III* and dictatorship, and (6) *The Tempest* and postcolonialism. The second option I called 'Global Shakespeare and local demons', which would follow a less strict format than the previous one. Starting from a general understanding of appropriations of Shakespeare within the context of a specific locality and cultural tradition, students would next choose a specific context (preferably based on their own background) and 'consider how Shakespeare productions engaged in addressing specific, context-bound dilemmas, the "local demons"'. In such an approach, both the historical, political and cultural context would be addressed and how these would find their ways into local productions. The course allowed students a fair amount of freedom to explore their own roots and also to learn from those of their fellow students. The third option I offered was titled 'Shakespeare and leadership'. This course built on my experience in the faculty of management and zoomed in on 'the insight his plays might offer in leadership issues by exploring two plays with contrasting leadership styles in more detail, *Henry V* and *Richard III*'. The course would include a textual analysis of the plays, a viewing of recent productions, and an analysis of the lessons that might (or might not) be learned from them and how these related to the broader discourses in society. Our conversation took place within the context of a pleasant, little café opposite the academy building and the chair of Humanities selected the third option, with the only proviso that I would change the title to 'Leadership in Culture', as it might draw more students. While to me it felt a slightly misleading title, this was a compromise I would have to make. The final step I needed to take was to send our selected and agreed-upon course proposal for approval to the chair of Social Sciences at the University College, which turned out to be a mere formality. The obstacles had been taken and I could embark on my next transdisciplinary project, 'Leadership in Culture'. It resulted in the following (abbreviated) course description for students.

3.1 Course Description for Students

Leadership in Culture

Over the past decades, scholars have increasingly argued the relevance of the humanities for leadership studies and society's pressing concerns. In particular, William Shakespeare, being the most read, translated, taught, and performed playwright, has been a source of inspiration, not only due to his status as a global icon, or to the seeming timelessness of his plays and topics, but also based on the ambiguity and multi-interpretability that pervade his plays. In this interdisciplinary course, we build on this and interrogate how his plays may offer useful insight into issues that are relevant for today's leaders. We do so by discussing two plays with contrasting leadership styles in more detail, *Henry V* and *Richard III*, as well as other plays that explore issues that are relevant for today's leaders. The course includes textual analysis of plays, the viewing of (parts of) recent productions, and a discussion on the specifics of leadership and today's challenges as seen through the lens of these plays and the lessons that may (or may not) be learned from them. In the course, students work together to interrogate the lessons, within a specific local or global context, and devise their own creative responses to Shakespeare's texts in a practical project. No previous knowledge of Shakespeare is required, as I will be your guide in this journey.

Hours per week	4
Number of weeks	9
Teaching method	Seminar
Assessment	Reflective Essay, Creative Group Project, Assignments, Participation
Course type	Bachelor
Student composition	Liberal arts and sciences (multidisciplinary); internationally diverse (25 per cent Dutch, 75 per cent international)
Number of instructors	1
ECTS	5

Learning Outcomes

By the end of this course, students will have:

1. Extended their ability to work across disciplines and build on the humanities to address challenges of twenty-first-century leaders, in both the political and the managerial arenas;
2. Learned to apply key concepts from leadership studies;
3. Deepened their critical awareness of how Shakespeare operates, and how the lessons that might be distilled from his plays and productions could be of relevance for today's leaders;
4. Applied their understanding of the relationship between Shakespeare and leadership in the development of a creative group project and practical performance work (e.g. 10 min adaptation, filmed);
5. Demonstrated their ability to reflect critically on their course work, the themes discussed in class, and their specific individual contribution to the student-devised practical project.

Output

1. Group Project (40 per cent). During the course, the students will be working on a project, in which they demonstrate their ability to apply an understanding of the relationship between Shakespeare, leadership and contemporary issues in the development of an audio-visual creative group project work (e.g. a production or a 10-min adaptation, filmed). The group project will also include a feedback session, in which the group analyses the effect of their creative work on their peers, how this relates to the intended effect of their project and what lessons may be learned from this. Assessment criteria include: audience awareness, subject knowledge, coherence, originality and creativity, visual attractiveness, relevance and structure. Presentation of the group project is in weeks 8–9.
2. Assignments (30 per cent). A variety of assignments are included in the course, which range from brief, written reports on readings, (partly) chairing or participating in a discussion, acting and directing, reflecting on the course, or critically interrogating provided reading material.

(cont.)

3. Participation (20 per cent). This aspect includes your active participation inside and outside the class, as in responses to in-class quizzes/questions, exhibition of professional behaviour (attendance, punctuality, informing valid absences), participation in Discussion Board on Nestor (both by way of intelligent questions and tips, raising useful topics, suggesting useful literature, and addressing/answering questions and topics that other students have introduced).
4. Written Report (10 per cent). This constitutes a written report in weeks 3–4 on the group project that the group aims at working on during the course. Assessment criteria include viability, creativity, interdisciplinarity and relevance.

3.2 Course Set-Up and Lectures

The course description was still relatively vague and also extended beyond the original plan that the chair and I had decided upon as I aimed at moving beyond the topic of leadership. Not surprisingly, I received an email from two students beforehand inquiring what we would actually be doing and requesting further clarification in order to help them determine whether or not to take the course:

> I am contacting you because I am interested in the course 'Leadership and Culture' that you will be teaching during semester IIb. I was wondering if you could send me the syllabus of the course, in order to better understand whether it suits my Major.
> In this regard, I am doing a collaborative Free-Major in Medical Humanities with my fellow student [name of student]. We are studying medicine from an anthropological perspective, by focusing on the (potential) role of Humanities in the medical practice.
> Would you suggest us to take the course?

As I was still in the process of developing the course (and did not have any syllabus as yet), I decided to reply positively by an extensive email (about the size of an A4) referring, amongst other things, to the transdisciplinary approach of the medical humanities, which builds on the lessons that the arts and humanities, but also the social sciences may offer to healthcare in the broadest sense of the word. At the same time, I mentioned that they could include medical and ethical challenges and dilemmas, based on Shakespeare's plays, in the final group assignment if they so wished. They replied as follows:

> Thank you so much for your thorough answer. We really appreciate that. The course sounds amazing and we completely agree with you when saying that the study of Shakespeare is of great usefulness in many fields, including medicine. We will definitely take your course into account. We will probably see you very soon.
> P.S. Thank you for the passage from *Macbeth*. I happen to know the tragedy very well, since it was the play at centre of my last year of high school. Unfortunately, at the time I didn't realize the connection between the psychological problems and the physical symptoms that Shakespeare makes in many of his works, as you rightly said.

They took the course and explored the narratives of love sickness and rape and its effect on women in their final project. The relatively loose approach I took in replying to these students' initial email fit in with the approach of the course as a whole which I had in mind: the first couple of weeks would be relatively fixed, whereas the second part of the course would allow students more freedom in exploring topics of their own choice.

At the start of the course, the Covid-19 pandemic broke out and the effect of this on the lectures, assignments and evaluations is interwoven in the text of Section 3. In order to find out to what extent the students' own personal interests and the more general course content could be brought productively together, I used the entire first lecture to discuss the background of the students, why they had chosen this course and what their interest in Shakespeare was. The specialisations of the students were varied and included psychology, philosophy, international relations, international business, politics, social change, medical humanities and the broad major arts and literature. The age range was between twenty and twenty-three (third year students) and their home countries included the Netherlands, Austria, the United Kingdom, France, Italy, Switzerland, Germany and Lithuania. Their reasons for choosing this elective varied: some of the reasons were very specific, such as a student who mentioned that he was 'writing a thesis about masculinity in self-help and this course seemed to allow for an alternative look on masculinity through the lens of Shakespeare and leadership'. Intriguingly, some students chose the course because of the very lack of specificity in the course description and the wide terrain it seemed to cover:

> I chose this course because I am curious. I appreciate the interdisciplinary courses, like this one. I really like the creative aspect of it, described in the course description, the project we will work on, etc . . . I find that very exciting. And it seems like an original course: Leadership – Culture – and Shakespeare . . . I don't know what to make of it now and it is really exciting.

Next to these, more specific reasons, a more general interest (or even passion in some cases) in literature, theatre and Shakespeare was what motivated students as well, with several referring to previous acting they had done at primary or secondary school and a desire to know more about Shakespeare. Another group expressed the interest they had in topics such as leadership and ethics and how this related to their future careers. Although the accents were different between students, most of them indicated that the combination of Shakespeare and leadership intrigued them. In hindsight, it seemed that the title for the course, which I had considered slightly misleading, turned out to be effective after all. Not for every student, though, as exemplified by this student's reaction:

> At first, when I saw the word 'leadership' in the title of the course, I immediately scrolled down as I find it

> repulsive. Though later, I decided to have a look at the course. When I started reading it, I found it truly interesting. I guess Shakespeare and the role plays made me forget about my distaste for the 'leadership' and really intrigued me. At the same time, I thought: what does leadership have to do with Shakespeare? I guess I'm purely driven by curiosity.

The curiosity of the students, their more general interest in crossing disciplines, combined with some quite specific reasons, such as the earlier mentioned student's interest in masculinity, offered me enough to work with in this course and next I was interested to gain an understanding of where they stood on Shakespeare. Although I had indicated in the course description that no previous knowledge of Shakespeare was required, it would be useful to have an idea of how much they did know and how I could I work with this. About half of the students had studied Shakespeare previously, but not extensively, having read two or three of his plays, seen some productions and adaptations and read some sonnets. About a quarter of the students had little knowledge of Shakespeare, generally having read no more than one play at most or performed in the odd secondary school production; all of them, however, expressed a desire to know more about the author and the plays. The final group, also comprising about a quarter, had more extensive knowledge of the playwright with some even having read most of his plays:

> I have read almost all his plays. In high school I was Helena in *Midsummer Night's Dream* and Lady Macbeth in *Macbeth*. My favourite play is *Hamlet*, it has everything: revenge, murder, Freudian relationships, madness.

As one of my aims in starting this course at the University College was to find a better balance between Shakespeare and social sciences, the current student composition seemed promising. The combination of enthusiasm and pre-existing knowledge on Shakespeare was a good starting point and the differences in backgrounds and specialisations, to a large extent from the social sciences, provided a helpful basis for exploring the interaction between Shakespeare and today's society. The basic set-up of the course had by now crystallised in my mind and during the second lecture I used the image of three juggling balls, as shown in Figure 1, to illustrate the concept.

Using this simplified representation as a starting point, the students were divided in three subgroups, each of which explored one of the three concepts in more detail. In particular, I asked them to consider aspects such as which topics they would address, which kind of teachers they would typically have, in what departments and disciplines they would generally be located. After coming together again, we discussed what kind of overlap there might be between the concepts, how they might benefit, supplement or challenge each other and, if so, how. During the course, we would continue to explore the relation between these concepts and in

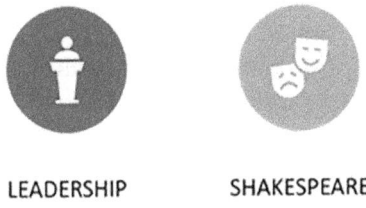

LEADERSHIP   SHAKESPEARE

21ST CENTURY
CHALLENGES

Figure 1 The juggling balls

order to bring the variety of levels in Shakespeare knowledge more in alignment, it would be necessary to create a safe environment in which students would be at ease and able to cooperate productively. The more advanced group would have to be challenged, while at the same time the others would be improving their ability to work with Shakespeare. As I had promised to work with *Henry V* in the course description, and as this was a play relatively unknown to most of the students, this offered a good starting point and I decided to use the first couple of weeks by focusing entirely on this one play. We worked in constantly shifting subgroups and to get everyone acquainted with the language, we started off with close reading from specific scenes at home, followed by presenting and discussing during lectures not only the content but also the present-day implications of these scenes. The selected scenes invariably included ethical or emotional dilemmas related to leadership, such as the decision to go to war, the traitors scene, the Harfleur ultimatum, the hanging of Bardolph, the Crispin speech, Henry's walk in disguise through the camp and the killing of the prisoners. We also took a step back at times and watched and compared movies and theatre productions of the play and engaged in literature review as well, zooming in on publications on Shakespeare, ethics and leadership (e.g. Branagh, 1989; Donaldson, 1991; Doran, 2015; Herbel, 2015; Leroy, 2012; Olivier, 1944; Rabkin, 1977; Robinson, 2016; Warner, 2007).

In an attempt to include watching a production together during Covid, I had asked my students to meet online at an agreed-upon time in the afternoon when everyone would be available for at least four hours in order to watch Gregory Doran's 2015 *Henry V* by the Royal Shakespeare Company. Using the online streaming service of Marquee TV, all students would watch the production from their own homes. We met online at 15.00, the agreed-upon starting time, and started with ten minutes for online pre-performance chats, after which we all started watching at the same time. After scene 3.7 there was a natural break, which we also took, and we paused for twenty minutes. I had asked the students to use the first five minutes of the break to write down their first impressions on the shared online platform. Next we took a refreshment break and discussed each other's comments online for fifteen minutes. Immediately after the second half of the production we would share further comments. Inevitably, watching under lockdown had a huge impact on the students' experiences, many of whom had indicated already that they experienced 'a higher level of anxiety', 'a lower mood', or being 'more sad than usual', caused by the quarantine and social distancing, the general negative mood and the closure of many of the venues they used to frequent.

In the assignment connected to the online viewing experience I had asked students 'to review this production not only as a regular production (including this course's perspective and your particular interest), but also to convey your unique experience of solitary (or family/friend) "theatre-going"'. All of the students indicated they would have preferred a live production, as exemplified by this student's reaction:

> In the past, my theatre experience has always involved going to the physical theatre itself. The *Teatro Signorelli*, the theatre of my hometown in Italy, is a special place for me; in fact, it could be called my second home. The viewing of Shakespeare's *Henry V* was my first experience with online 'theatre going'; and coming from my past experience, it was interesting to view a theatre performance from my student apartment as if it were a movie.
>
> This being said, I missed out on the experience of *actually* going to theatre with my friends, of the theatre going rituals such as booking tickets, getting ready to go to theatre and perhaps having a drink before the show. These are all rituals that I did not recreate as I did not feel the necessity to do so. After all, for me personally, a screen cannot substitute the experience of 'theatre going' as I know it.

At the same time, the students appreciated the possibility of being able to chat online in the break and immediately after a production and mentioned benefits such as having access to subtitles, being able to watch expressions of actors, used as most of them were to the cheaper seats further back from the stage, and also of being in the comfort of one's own home with the advantages such as 'sitting on my comfortable sofa and [having] time to make myself a hot chocolate during the break'. Students discussed 'the decision to place more burden on the words spoken than action enacted [which] encouraged the audience to not only listen, but hear and feel the forceful and potent dialogue' and Alex Hassell's 'portraying a multifaceted Henry'. More surprisingly, many of the reviews also expressed the students' surprise at the humour of the production, something they had not experienced while reading: '[It] set in motion something which I did not expect from this play: I was laughing!' Also scene 2.3, Pistol's leave-taking of Nell, highly impressed the students, something I myself could relate to as well as it was, from a screening perspective, an unmistakable highlight of the production. Within the constraints set by Covid, students indicated they enjoyed watching the production, as exemplified in this student's reaction: '[It] actually made me want to watch more of Shakespeare's plays, [even though] it cannot replace seeing a play live in the theatre.' The initial focus in the course on one play and one topic in particular depth allowed the group to come closer together in knowledge and was also intended to lay the groundwork for how one might explore a play by Shakespeare within the context of other twenty-first-century challenges.

After this introductory and relatively fixed start to the course, we took one more week to consider other possible challenges and plays, with students discussing *Richard 3* & Donald Trump, *Othello* & racial discourse and *The Taming of the Shrew* & the #MeToo movement. In the next phase of the course, students formed groups with similar interests, based on the twenty-first-century challenges they wanted to address. On a timeline, the course looked roughly like indicated in Figure 2.

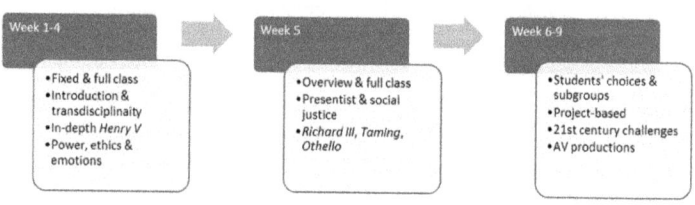

Figure 2 Timeline leadership in culture

The sessions from week six onwards were small-scale and group-based and would result in the final audiovisual productions. The length of each production would be approximately 10 minutes, they would be shown in the online classroom and afterwards the students would engage in a twenty- to thirty-minute discussion on the production, the responses it elicited from the other students, its intended goals and the extent to which the production had achieved its aims or had gone beyond that. The first group explored the depiction of love sickness in general in *Twelfth Night* and *As You Like It*, and next focused on the characters Phaedra (in *Hippolytus* by Euripides) and the Jailer's Daughter (*Two Noble Kinsmen*), further exploring the themes of lovesickness and rape. Inspired by Neely's *Distracted Subjects* (2018) and Rackin's *Shakespeare and Women* (2005) and building on literature from the social sciences (e.g. Garcia, 2012; Gilman et al., 1993; McNamara, 2016; Toohey, 2004), they connected the two plays and characters with some of the myths of love sickness and rape throughout history that still affect today's society. It resulted in a final project that, in the words of the student group, told the story of 'the unrecognized female sufferer; victim of a male narrative that still to this day has dramatic consequences'.

> The question we ask is: POSSUM FUGERE? (*Translation:* Can we escape this?). Will we, women, ever be free from the narratives that, even today, take us away from our right to safety, respect and recognition as equal human beings?

They expressed these topics by way of a mesmerising body paint adaptation. The bodies of the students gradually changed colour, caused by their own and other hands. Accompanied by Shakespeare texts, 'the movement of mutual body-paint represents both the internal and external struggles and pressures by society at large and the opposite sex', the student group commented.

The second group decided to zoom in on class divide with relation to Shakespeare and performance. Whereas in early modern times all levels of society attended, the students argued that nowadays a class divide had arisen with regard to Shakespeare productions. They employed the popular template of *Crash Course* (2011 et seq.) YouTube videos, who partnered with Arizona State University from 2020 onwards, in order to address this imbalance and make Shakespeare more accessible for a wider twenty-first-century audience. Acting out scenes from *Henry V* and *Romeo and Juliet*, which they interspersed with talk-show student presenters, they aimed to demonstrate how these two plays could be used to address present-day concerns. They did so through the use of modern slang and modern scenery in a popular talk-show setting, while introducing topics they considered to be high on the popular agenda, such as corporate greed (in *Henry V*) and Covid (in *Romeo and Juliet*).

The final project focused on gender roles and took *The Taming of the Shrew* as the point of departure. In their project proposal, the students wrote that the aim of the project was to:

> examine how contemporary audiences react to it [*The Taming of the Shrew*] when presented with explicit performances of exaggerated gendered domination on stage. By doing so, we aimed to show that Shakespeare can be an 'agent of change', and by depicting social constructs to audiences, he is able to show their absurdity and invite play-goers to criticize them.

They acted out and filmed part of scene 2.1, with a gender reversal in the middle of the scene: at first Petruchio was played by a male student and Katherine by a female student, but halfway through the scene the roles changed resulting in the gender reversal. In the project proposal, the students argued that they chose this scene because of the 'similarities of a setting which one could encounter nowadays in any bar or nightclub: A man thinks he is entitled to a woman because he buys her a drink and commences to pursue her. Oftentimes her reaction can be ambivalent and misunderstood by the man'. Not unexpectedly for social sciences students, they also employed quantitative research by combining questions about their video with a questionnaire on dating experiences, which they sent out to other students (not participating in the course) of the University College together with the

AV production they had made. A total of fifty-three students participated in this research, the results of which were included in the AV production. One of the surprising results, as worded in the group's reflection report, was that 'most women saw the scene in a negative light, while men mostly perceived it as a scene with a neutral tone'. Following the (online) classroom discussion, the student group reflected how it was 'troublesome that essences of this 'dating norm' where women are prizes to be pursued and won from Shakespeare's era remained ingrained in contemporary society'.

3.3 Aftermath
3.3.1 Grading

Whereas in the previous course I was constricted both by a pre-determined structure, end product and assessment criteria, in this course I was able to determine the products and the assessment criteria myself, which I had communicated to the students beforehand (see discussion under course description). The AV project and other class assignments figured most prominently, weighing for 80 per cent in the grade, with participation weighing 20 per cent. The Dutch grading system is based on a scale which runs from one to ten. A student passes a course if the grade is six or higher. The grade ten is rarely awarded for theses or related assignments (in all my years, I have never come across it). The grade nine is very good (and is required for a summa cum laude distinction), an eight equals good (and is required for a cum laude distinction), the grade seven is standard, six below standard (but still a pass, just). The grades five and lower are unsatisfactory to very poor. On this course, three students scored a nine, the remainder was awarded an eight. To this day, grading is a hotly debated topic in education research and one about which differences of opinion continue to exist with authors arguing that rather than providing definitive answers, there is an ongoing need for serious discussions about grading approaches, expectations, and communications (Guskey & Brookhart, 2019; Smith & Smith, 2019; Townsley, 2022). In this course, a combination of learning goals, regular and specific feedback on product, process and progress, providing multiple grades on four different categories (participation, project proposal, class assignments and AV production) and student feedback were used to support the grading. The final grades were not given until after the student evaluations had been handed in to avoid any possible correlation between the two. While I had tried to be as precise as possible, using a scale from ten to one hundred, allocating points for each of the four categories and dividing them by ten, I was somewhat uneasy by the grading, as no other persons were involved in the process. This was something that I would prefer to (and did) address in a future course as my feedback was now limited to those of the students.

3.3.2 Student Evaluation

The student evaluations, which they had to fill in before the grading but after the lectures, were anonymous and, to my delight, quite extensive. This first year of the course had felt as somewhat of an experiment, and I was hoping that the anonymity would allow for honest and critical feedback in order to improve my course. During the course itself, a student suggested that 'after the George Floyd incident and the protests, *Othello* would be an appropriate play to analyse in more detail as it touches upon racism'. This was a valuable suggestion, as the play had only been given very limited time in the course. Later on, this turned out to be a suggestion which found its way into the course description of the third transdisciplinary course I taught (Section 4) and also into the content of the fourth transdisciplinary course (Section 5). In the evaluation reports, one student remarked they would have 'appreciated to hear more from the prof and less from my fellow students'. While I consider student discussion to be an unmissable part of any course, there were times when I itched to enter the debate more. Perhaps I should be less cautious here; it is an aspect that I could monitor better during the course itself. Possibly the lack of experience with online-teaching (at times, I did feel like an amateur in this respect) might also have played a role here. Another student indicated that the course objectives were not described clearly. A just remark, as the course objectives, which were vague anyway, shifted somewhat during the course due to the set-up, which allowed for students to explore those elements of the terrain that were of particular interest to them. This was something that I could clarify better in the following year. A final point of attention was the effect of Covid, which struck in the year of the course, due to which I had to change some assignments:

> Thank you very much for teaching this course this block. I think it is a real shame that it came in the block affected by corona as it is difficult to appreciate Shakespeare without performance. I think you came up with innovative ways to get around these difficulties and, as a student, I appreciated it a lot.

Content-wise, the students considered the course to be a mixture of fun and learning and reflected positively on the interaction between the humanities and the social sciences, a central element in the course, as exemplified by this student reaction:

> I really enjoyed your course as it was something quite different from all the other courses I have taken as a business student. I think I will remember this project (and course) as something unique that is out of my comfort zone, yet very interesting. I was rather content about our final deliverable we presented and believe I have acquired exclusive knowledge on the relationship between Shakespeare, leadership and societal issues. It is remarkable how something that is written in the sixteenth century is still relevant to help us understand our society.

Some of the responses discussed not only the course, the assignments or the relation between Shakespeare and present-day challenges in society, but also the effect the course had on a personal level. These personal reactions and how Shakespeare might affect a human being touched me more than anything:

> I found myself in a toxic relationship with someone who did not want me to pursue my studies and whom I had let destroy the perception I had of myself and my self-worth. [...] I found myself surprised to feel so close to Shakespeare,

and recognised myself in 'The Taming of the Shrew'. The play acted like a mirror to my own life, my emancipation. It reminded me of who I am, of my essence. Shakespeare is everywhere... I was surprised to see that he was born on the same day as me, centuries ago. Whether you believe in God or not, there is no doubt that this course came just in time and in a way, saved me. I will be forever grateful for this.

I can still see myself reading this student's evaluation with a lump in my throat. In a way, this one student's experience had made it all worth it.

3.3.3 Compromises

In reaching out to non-English literature students in this new transdisciplinary course, I had addressed several of the concerns I had experienced at the faculty of management. In the new course, I had been able to introduce a variety of assignments, specifically geared to the transdisciplinarity I was aiming for, the student composition had become more diverse, the topic of the course now went beyond leadership and included other topics of social justice as well and last but not least, the course provided a better balance between on the one hand an appreciation of Shakespeare and on the other hand an understanding of the relationship with relevant topics within the field of social justice. While the students' (and my own) enthusiasm stimulated me to continue and further refine this course, which I did over the next few years, there were also some aspects that proved harder to change within the context of the present course at this faculty. The title, Leadership in Culture, was a non-negotiable element, which made it difficult for me to shift the course right from the start of the lectures towards social justice topics in general. Another point of contention was that I taught and graded the course by myself, and while I have a broad, multidisciplinary background, a transdisciplinary course on Shakespeare and social justice might benefit further from a combination of teachers coming from different disciplines. Finally, taking to heart the student's comment earlier about it being difficult to 'appreciate Shakespeare without performance', I started considering options how to include this in the course (post-Covid, of course). However, at the current faculty there was no budget to allow, for example, for trips to English-spoken productions. All of these considerations led me to develop and teach a new course for another faculty at our university, the Honours College Groningen.

4 Transdisciplinary Teaching: Shakespeare, Social Justice and Collaboration

Faculty: Honours College (offers students an extra bachelor degree programme, focused on broadening their knowledge, which students can take in addition to their regular bachelor programme), University of Groningen.

The course 'Leadership in Culture' had already moved towards (or perhaps even beyond) the type of courses that I had envisioned when I had only just started on the journey towards teaching transdisciplinary Shakespeare to non-English literature students. At the same time, by now I had also achieved a clearer picture of the compromises and difficulties involved in this process and I found myself considering options to address three of these concerns in particular. First, I would prefer to collaborate with other teachers as well, preferably with different academic or professional backgrounds, to further enhance the transdisciplinarity of the course (and also to ensure that my grading was correct). Second, I wanted to have the focus of the course more explicitly on topics of social justice. Finally, notwithstanding a student's remarks that I had found 'innovative ways to get around these difficulties', I wanted them to get a more 'real-life' experience of Shakespeare performance to better appreciate not only his plays but also how they interacted with social justice topics. Again, this would require some serious thinking and energy on my part, but buoyed by the success of the previous course, I continued the journey towards transdisciplinarity and decided upon the Honours College. This is a faculty at the University of Groningen where students can take an extra bachelor degree programme in addition to their regular bachelor programme. No more than 300 students per year are allowed to follow the programme, and only highly motivated students are granted access. The faculty stresses that the 'interdisciplinary approach will be very important, next to intensifying the knowledge of your own degree programme. Together with other students from all faculties, you will look into scientific and social issues from different disciplinary angles' (Honours, 2023).

As luck would have it, and sometimes one needs a bit of luck in this process, at the very moment I was considering the Honours College, the Dean happened to publish a blog on the university's intranet. In the blog the Dean referred to the university's strategy and the benefits of working across disciplines in teaching and research:

> 'A broader perspective broadens one's thinking.' A wise quote by Loesje (if you don't know who Loesje is, look her up on Google some time). This quote is also valuable for academia: looking beyond the borders of your own discipline can enrich your knowledge. Collaboration between disciplines is also valuable for solving complex societal problems. In the upcoming Strategic Plan, more extensive interdisciplinary cooperation in research and teaching will be stimulated. (Elzinga, 2020)

As I dug a little deeper, I also came across the publication of the inaugural lecture of the Dean on accepting the post of Professor in Development and Differentiation in Academic Education, with a special emphasis on paths of excellence in an interdisciplinary context (Elzinga, 2014). This seemed like too good an opportunity to pass up and I sent an email of some ten lines, responding to her blog, indicating my interest in teaching within a transdisciplinary context such as the Honours College, my own multi-disciplinary background and referring to a publication on Shakespeare, blackface and race (Heijes, 2020) by way of an example. The return mail (also some ten lines) arrived a couple of days later and in it the Dean expressed her curiosity, which led her to look up the publication and read parts of it: 'You approach a topical and relevant theme from different angles. That you include the theatre (Othello) is very interesting to me.' She invited me to have a chat as this was the kind of teaching they would be interested in at the Honours College.

After a couple of conversations, including the Vice Dean and the Education Coordinator, we agreed upon a transdisciplinary course on

Shakespeare and social justice which addressed my main concerns. First, it was agreed that other lecturers would be allowed in the course as well, provided that I would be the course coordinator and the main teacher. At my request, two teachers were added to the course. A teacher from the section of social sciences, specialisation pedagogy, would be included to provide a guest lecture, attend some other lectures, assist in the grading and participate in the summer school. For the second part of the course (year 3) a teacher in theatre studies from outside the University would be included to assist in working towards an envisioned final theatre production. Both of them brought in specific knowledge, the perspective of a different discipline and checks on my grading and teaching in general. In addition, both of them had experience in working with Shakespeare as well, the first teacher had taught English at secondary school for some fifteen years, before moving on to academia, the second teacher was also a professional director and had directed Shakespeare before. Regarding my other concern, including more 'real-life' experience of Shakespeare, we agreed on two specific aspects. First, a budget would be provided to allow for visiting course-related, English-spoken theatre productions with the students, provided the students would pay one third of the costs themselves. Second, the course would also include a short theatre production, written and performed by the students and based on the expertise they had garnered during the course. In order to fit this rather ambitious and time-consuming course within the curriculum, we decided to turn it into a two year's course (taught during the second and third year of the bachelor). Visualised on a timeline, the course would look roughly as in Figure 3.

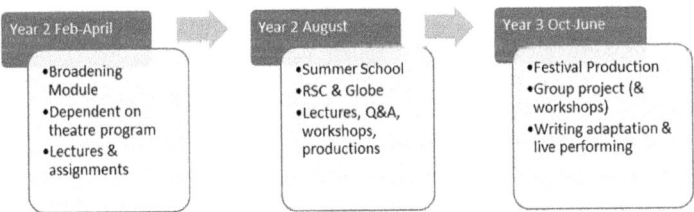

Figure 3 Timeline of 'The Upstart Crow'

The title of this new course, open to Honours College students from all faculties, would be 'The Upstart Crow: #BLM, #MeToo, #Trump', resulting in the following course description.

4.1 Course Description for Students

The Upstart Crow: #BLM, #MeToo, #Trump

Over the past decades, the boundaries between the social sciences and the arts and humanities have slowly begun to erode as scholars have increasingly argued the relevance of the arts and humanities in tackling social problems. In particular, William Shakespeare, being the most read, translated, taught and performed playwright ever, has been a source of inspiration, not only due to his status as a global icon, or to the seeming timelessness of his plays and topics, but also based on his keen insight in human nature and the ambiguity and multi-interpretability that pervade his plays.

Recently, the most prestigious business schools have started to explore ways of drawing on the richness of Shakespeare's plays in order to shed light on challenges that leaders face today. Barack Obama and Nelson Mandela considered Shakespeare foundational to their thinking, while Angela Merkel considered his plays invaluable for understanding autocrats. More popular today than ever, his plays are used worldwide to address #BLM, #MeToo and #Trump in 140 countries, including many countries where English is not the official language. The uses to which his plays are put are endless, ranging from fostering dissidence to autocracy to helping veterans, struggling with PTSD, or inmates in high-security prisons to develop life skills that ensure their successful integration into society.

In this course we build on this by employing a convergence approach to scholarship, reaching across disciplines to address pressing social challenges. Through a selection of plays and adaptations, we study how these address today's burning issues, how they inform our thinking and what we may learn from them. Topics we may explore include

(cont.)

racism, sexism, gender-specificity, autocracy, religious conflict, social justice, reintegration and dissidence within a specific local or global context.

This broadening module lays the groundwork for a Summer School visit to the UK, during which we visit London and Stratford-upon-Avon, Shakespeare's birthplace. We will see some of the most renowned theatre companies perform his plays, sharpen our skills of critical observation and reflection, and discuss the impact and relevance with specialists in the field. In year three, students further specialise in and interrogate twenty-first-century challenges of their own interest. They devise their own creative responses to these challenges, building on Shakespeare's plays or adaptations, in a practical, theatrical project which will be presented live at a festival in the main Academy Building to a wider audience.

Odd as it may seem, a knowledge of Shakespeare, also known as the Upstart Crow, is not a prerequisite as I will be your guide on that part of the journey. No, in the end, what matters most, what matters only, is a positive answer to the following questions:

> *Do you really want to work across disciplines?*
> *Do you want to tackle today's challenges?*
> *You sure you're not afraid of a challenge?*
> *In that case, I look very much forward to working with you.*

Hours per week	variable (2–4)
Number of weeks	7 (year 2), 1 week Summer School, 14 (year 3)
Teaching method	Seminar and Summer School
Assessment	Reflective Essay, Group and Individual Assignments, Participation, Final Production Project
Course type	Bachelor

(cont.)	
Student composition	Multidisciplinary and international (natural sciences, social sciences and humanities students; 20 per cent Dutch, 80 per cent international)
Number of instructors	7 (including 4 summer school teachers)
ECTS	10

4.2 Course Set-Up and Lectures

At my request, the course started in semester 2.1 (the Dutch academic year has two semesters, running respectively from September to mid-January and from mid-February to June; each semester is split into two different sections). The reason for starting mid-February was intrinsically linked with the set-up of the course: the end of January, start of February sees the announcement of the theatre programmes of the RSC and the Globe. By then, I would also know the number of students, allowing me to buy tickets for productions before the general sale would open (avoiding any unpleasantness of sold-out productions). At the same time, it would allow me (just enough) time to start preparing the lectures and give the students (just enough) time to do some preliminary reading. It was cutting it close though. The questions the students asked me before the start of the course related mainly to the required Shakespeare knowledge (which I could answer to a certain extent), to the plays we would study (which I could not yet answer as the summer season schedules had not yet been announced) and to the assignments they would be required to do (which I had difficulty answering, as they depended in part on the specific plays). While I was able to explain both the potential benefits and challenges of the course, in part based on my previous experiences, I also wished I could have been more specific. However, due to the set-up of the course this was not possible as the plays (and henceforth also the themes) would be determined by the as yet unknown RSC and Globe scheduling. In a sense, I was asking all of these students to go down the rabbit hole with me. Fortunately, they were not put off by the uncertainties and the course was oversubscribed (the Honours College guarantees relatively small-sized classes of no more than twenty to twenty-five students).

The academic backgrounds of the students were even more varied than at the University College, as they now encompassed the entire spectrum: social sciences, art and humanities and physical sciences with majors including international business, history, psychology, European language and culture, international relations, international law, biology, industrial engineering and life science and technology. The nationality of the students was also more diverse and now extended beyond Europe, including Germany, Iran, Bulgaria, the United Kingdom, Italy, Austria, Romania, Ecuador, the Netherlands, South Africa and Belarus. Some of their reasons for joining the course were very specific, as in the case of an international law student:

> I have always loved reading Shakespeare's sonnets but truth be told have never managed to read or study any of his plays. When this class came up it seemed just like too good of an opportunity to pass by.

Most reasons for choosing the course differed not so much from those of the previous two courses: wanting 'to broaden my mind', 'fondly remembering drama classes at secondary school', 'missing arts and the theatre' or simple curiosity. The students' ages ranged between nineteen and twenty-four and their knowledge of Shakespeare was slightly lower than the class at the University College but higher than the one at the Faculty of Economics and Business. Almost all of them had read (often in translation), seen and/or acted in one (or more) of his plays, while a couple had previous directing experience. What further bound these students was a desire to challenge themselves beyond the confines of their traditional discipline and also an ambition to excel both in and after their studies.

In February we kicked off with the first part of the course, the broadening module, which would lay the groundwork for the following summer school in the UK and the student theatre production in the year after. Two weeks before the course started, the RSC and the Globe published their summer season schedule and as the summer school was scheduled for the second half of August, the selected plays would be *Much Ado About Nothing* and *Richard III* at the Royal Shakespeare Theatre and *All's Well That Ends Well* and *I, Joan* (Josephine, 2022) at the Globe Theatre. Due to scheduling constraints, we could only choose three Shakespeare productions and had to include the modern play *I, Joan* (loosely based on Joan of Arc) as well. While it was not my original intention to do so and while the course focused on Shakespeare, in hindsight it worked out quite well not only as a foil but also as an interesting twenty-first-century production in itself and the students integrated it neatly into their final theatre production. The three Shakespeare plays were the main focus of the course and gave me more than enough to work with on relevant, present-day challenges and over the next two weeks (for which I had carefully kept a relatively clean agenda, free of other activities) I further developed the course and the assignments.

4.2.1 Broadening Module

Fortunately, the Covid-19 restrictions had been lifted by now and I was able to choose a far more differentiated approach by way of teaching. As I had only seven two-hour lecture weeks (instead of the nine four-hour lecture weeks of the University College), I had to devise a way to not only get this diverse group of students to read and appreciate Shakespearean texts and productions, but also to prepare them for watching and being able to discuss real-life productions, while simultaneously connecting them to recognisable twenty-first-century challenges. Discussing the conundrum with my co-teacher, we decided not to choose a final product, essay or other type of exam, but to work with a pressure-cooker approach: everything would be happening within the timeframe of the seven lecture-weeks during which students would work weekly in constantly shifting groups to engage with the relevance of Shakespearean texts and productions and discussing them with their peers. This meant that we would ask a lot of the students during the course, rather than at the end of it, on top of the fact that they could not prepare well in advance of the course, because the plays were known only shortly before the course started.

At the end of the course, one of the students also pointed this out in the course evaluation:

> I must admit that at first I was a little bit annoyed by the weekly group assignments as they require a lot of coordination. Nevertheless, they helped to a) get to know the group and other students so much better, b) engage intensively with the course material and deeply read the script, c) improve our presentation skills (after this long Corona period), d) try out new and challenging assignments such as 'acting', and e) work on our time management. [...] It was stressful but enriching, funny, and interesting.

After the introductory lecture, we started with *Much Ado About Nothing* engaging in close reading, some light acting and also discussing two movies (Branagh, 1993; Whedon, 2012), a televised production (Percival, 2005) and a theatre production (Leon, 2019), all the while considering to what extent they connected to social justice topics including gender, identity, sexism, abusive conduct and also racial discourse, the latter in the production by Kenny Leon (2019). The next play, *Richard III*, was originally intended to relate to the topic of autocracy, power, hate and Donald Trump, but at the start of the lectures Ukraine was invaded and we switched the focus also to Vladimir Putin, as this was very much on the students' minds, also on a very personal level in the student from Belarus, whose family lived close to the border. For sensitive topics such as these, a 'safe classroom' is of paramount importance in order for everyone to be able to express themselves, as reiterated by many students afterwards in the evaluation:

> The teacher and my fellow students have created a sense of community and belonging in this course that made me feel safe to participate in the discussions.

The importance of 'safe spaces' within the academic community, where students experience a sense of belonging in their academic classroom has long been considered an important factor positively associated with the students' experiences and results in the classroom (Freeman, Anderman & Jensen, 2007; Holley & Steiner, 2005). Likewise, the importance of 'brave spaces' has been highlighted as an important factor in allowing students to (respectfully) express their sometimes contrasting opinions (Palfrey, 2017). Some of the practical strategies that I have employed in my classroom to further this sense of community, belonging and respect were physical, such as working in a classroom where students could all see each other without feeling cramped. Also, first thing I do is ask students their names, what country they are from, hobbies, which specialisation they pursue and likewise questions. Beyond sheer human interest, knowing some basic facts about students and memorising their names (and pronouncing them correctly in an international group) right from the start has also been pointed out as contributing to a sense of being welcome (O'Brien, Leiman & Duffy, 2014). Some other strategies include promoting group work (students work together in changing subgroups), showing how mistakes are learning opportunities and owning my own mistakes as well, greeting students as they enter, having brief one-on-one conversations in the break, encouraging participation and allowing for freedom and student suggestions within the course.

Examples of assignments that we included in the broadening module included acting out the trial of Richard III, whom we imagined had survived the battle in Act 5. Students played prosecutor, defence, judge, Richard III, other character witnesses from the play and a jury, based on a setting of the International Criminal Court in The Hague. Another assignment focused on discussing the concept of 'power' and 'hate', which we explored by drawing parallels between *Richard III* and scenes from *THUG* (*The Hate U Give*) (Tillman, 2018) and the movie *Les Misérables* (Ly, 2019). In the final lectures we moved to *All's Well That Ends Well* and by now students were able to challenge themselves further by directing and performing the final scene (5.3) of the play in what was arguably the most complex assignment so far in terms of execution, cooperation and communication. It involved a student team of three directors and twelve actors, with the other students being the audience paying not only attention to the directorial vision and its relevance but also to the non-verbal communication and mini-narratives on stage, and how they strengthened, complicated or even subverted the main action going on at the same time.

4.2.2 Summer School

During the summer school (24–30 August 2022) the students attended *All's Well That Ends Well* and *Richard III* in Stratford-upon-Avon (RSC) and *Much Ado About Nothing* and *I, Joan* in London (Globe). Lectures and discussion with external teachers (actors, directors and academics) focused on the specific productions, on acting, directing and performance history and on present-day relevance and were facilitated by the Shakespeare Birthplace Trust and by Professor Pete Smith, which made for interesting new insights (on both sides) when confronted with the varied disciplinary backgrounds of the students. The scene, for example, where Paroles is being blindfolded and tricked into thinking he is being shot drew laughter from the audience, which only increased the sense of unease most students felt about presenting this bullying on stage: 'Making a comedy out of bullying Paroles made me feel uncomfortable.' This in turn led to input from the psychology students about the nature of laughter and how it can be expression of a variety of different emotions. Next, the law students pitched in from their perspective and launched a fierce attack on the scene in this production:

> I've been working a whole semester on torture for my studies in Armenia and what happened yesterday with Paroles on the stage falls fully under the definition of torture. Maybe you can show it, but not in a comic way. You wouldn't do a rape scene on stage and make people laugh, would you? [...] At the least, you should put out a warning beforehand; I mean, a scene like this can be very confrontational for a person suffering from PTSD.

Intriguingly, academic reviews paid almost no attention at all to the brutal nature of the torture scene, only briefly referring to it as the 'exposure of a coward' (Green, 2023) or the 'disorientation inflicted on a blindfolded Paroles' (Greenhalgh, 2024). Only Kirwan's review (2023) took it more seriously, discussing the effect it had on 'a distraught and traumatized

Parolles'. This review, however, was based on the film version of the play which seemingly enhanced the torture element with 'cameras [which] stare down the barrels of their guns' and 'a series of abusive and critical comments on the videos from those on social media who had watched the whole thing' (Kirwan, 2023). Similar discussions on the production were held about the bed-trick (or rape scene) with Bertram, which students felt could have been explored in more depth or in the words of a student: 'Instead of getting into the controversial topics, they skirted it.' It was intriguing (and rewarding) to see these students, coming from such different academic disciplines, engage in quite a few fierce discussions with actors, directors and academics, all of them well versed in Shakespeare. Taking a backseat during these sessions, I suppose I silently felt quite proud of them.

4.2.3 Festival Production

The group by now had a strong cohesion, coming through the pressure cooker of the broadening module and the summer school in the UK, and in the final part of the course they would work towards a theatre production building on the plays they had discussed and seen. Writing a thirty-minute Shakespeare adaptation, addressing challenges of the twenty-first century, co-directing the play and acting it out in front of a live audience in the main Academy Building in the centre of Groningen: this would truly be an ultimate challenge and the final achievement with which they would round off not only this course, but also their bachelor in the Honours programme. For this part of the course I was assisted by a co-teacher, a theatre director who had studied both in Basque Country and in London and had now been working for several years in the Netherlands, both on student productions and as a director for one of the main subsidised theatre companies in the Netherlands. In order to assist the students in the project, we offered on the one hand basic acting skills, which would be useful when performing for a live audience. At the same time, we had to whittle down the many ideas about the possible production. The students wanted to base their production on *Richard III*, *Much Ado About Nothing* and *I, Joan* and after two sessions on similarities, emotions and topics they wanted to explore the group was split up in three subgroups, with each group working on a fifteen- to twenty-minute script for their part, after which the whittling process continued to create an ultimate script merging them together. As the audience's knowledge of Shakespeare and these plays would be relatively limited, we decided to work with a two-person chorus who introduced the play and provided further comments during the production: they would welcome the audience at the festival, explain how they had modified three parts of the chosen plays, and indicate the throughline, moving from past to present while engaging with love and war. In the words of a draft script of the students:

> We start out with physical war, autocracy (Putinesque) and (lack of) love in *Richard III* > we move to love and war (soldiers are coming back from war, but also warring lovers) in *Much Ado* > we move back to physical war and love (of country, ideals) in *I, Joan*, reminiscent perhaps of a war being fought right now in Ukraine.

The language chosen for the production alternated between present-day English, included because the majority of the audience would not understand enough of the original text (except for *I, Joan*), and original parts of the text either because they were deemed accessible enough or because of their iconic status, such as the opening lines of *Richard III*. The production was accompanied by live piano and violin music of two students, and near the end, amidst the dead bodies on stage and the final words of Joan, the piano started some fragments, pianissimo, from the protest song *À la Volonté du Peuple*, which had first featured in the musical *Les Misérables* (Boublil & Schönberg, 1980), an adaptation of which, as mentioned before, was studied in the broadening module in exploring *Richard III* and the themes of hate and power. After the final words were spoken and Joan has also fallen, the script read:

> The violin now joins in and with the piano plays the melody of '*À la Volonté du Peuple*' as the bodies on the ground slowly stand up, while softly singing along with the music. The bodies form a line, hand in hand, in front of the audience, also joined now by the two presenters and Joan, who stands up as last and joins the line in the middle. All actors round off

with a final couplet, starting softly and swelling in volume and staring straight ahead, without blinking.

For both productions the chosen location in the main Academy Building was filled to the brim and many people wanting to see it had to be disappointed. For the students it was the desired grand finale of their Honours bachelor and for us, as teachers, it was the end of an inspiring two-year course in which students of so many different disciplines had come together to study transdisciplinary Shakespeare.

4.3 Aftermath
4.3.1 Grading

Considering my steps into transdisciplinary Shakespeare were still relatively new, I had preferred to have more persons involved in the grading process which was, as discussed before, one of the reasons for having more teachers involved in the course as grading was largely based on classroom activities. The grades for the broadening module and summer school were roughly the same as those for the previous course at the University College Groningen with one exception: there was no differentiation between the grades. The co-teacher, originating from social sciences and pedagogy, argued that the set-up of the course, the active participation of all students in presenting and discussing and the constantly shifting assignment groups warranted the high grade of eight (required for cum laude) for all students, with which I fully agreed. On grading the theatre production element of the course, the theatre director was also of the opinion that the intense process and the ultimate product merited the high grade of an eight, although the director argued that five students had gone so far beyond the call of duty, in terms of time investment, that they merited the exceptionally high grade of a nine. These were the student stage manager (who had throughout been an invaluable help in coordinating practical details), the chorus presenters and the two musicians (who had devised, composed and executed the music accompanying the production). While there were small differences of nuance in the grading process, my grades and those of both co-teachers aligned quite well which put my mind at rest about the validity of my grading.

4.3.2 Student Evaluation

The anonymous student evaluations at the Honours College were a mixture of quantitative and qualitative reports. The quantitative reports addressed six questions: (1) if the course delivered what one might expect from an Honours Class, (2) if different disciplinary student backgrounds were inspiring, (3) if the course was well organised, (4) if the assignments were well chosen, (5) if the course material was relevant and (6) if the class environment was safe. The maximum grade is five and the average of these six is the overall grade for the course. The student scores on five of these questions were between four and five and our course scored higher on all questions than the other courses, except for the third question on organisation, which 'only' scored a 3.4, which put it somewhere between neutral and agree. This did not entirely surprise me: I had had only a fortnight to prepare the course in detail and provide students with a reading list, it was my first year and the assignments were being developed as the course progressed, and finally, several of the classes ran overtime. These were challenges to be addressed in the next year. The overall score of the course was a 4.5, with the sixth question on a safe class environment being the highest and scoring a 4.8.

Fortunately the evaluation also provided very extensive qualitative feedback, which tends to be more specific and thus more helpful for me as a teacher. Some students were hesitant about the course due to earlier and less positive experiences with studying canonical literature and indicated how the variation in assignments helped them to appreciate the course:

> The Upstart Crow has triumphed above all expectations I initially held. When I put this course as my first choice, I was initially slightly hesitant. This was due to my bad experience with Dutch literature courses during high school, where the emphasis laid on (over)interpreting a dusty Dutch tome. Fortunately, this course has proven itself to be everything my Dutch literature courses should have been but were not. A fascinating course where there's a healthy balance between interpreting and studying the script and

> a practical application where our freedom could be expressed and our emotions liberated through acting.

While what the student refers to as '(over)interpreting a dusty Dutch tome' could for me very well be a useful and even energising close reading analysis, it is clear that for non-English literature students we cannot automatically assume that they appreciate these type of exercises as much as we do. I had selected a different approach and the choice for a high variety of carefully prepared group assignments worked quite well, even if it asked students to regularly step out of their comfort zone. For this, above all, a sense of togetherness and safety was paramount and acknowledged by the students, not only with a score of 4.8 in the quantitative result, but also in the many qualitative responses, such as the following one:

> In no moment I felt unable to participate, excluded or stupid. Enabling students to take part in a course with this atmosphere did not only help to engage easier with the course material but to feel comfortable stepping out of my comfort zone at any time.

Just as in the previous courses, during this course too some students indicated that the effects would also be noticeable beyond the course: 'I really enjoyed the course. I will definitely read more of his plays on my own.' My own personal pleasure in (teaching) Shakespeare and engaging with these transdisciplinary classes also seemed to be contagious and a student wrote: 'The professor was incredibly excited about the subject which made me excited as well.' The power of our own personal enthusiasm in teaching a subject about which we obviously care so much is not to be underestimated. Many studies on the relation between intrinsic teacher enthusiasm and student attention, motivation and achievement have found positive effects, although intriguingly teachers who had been trained to be enthusiastic failed to show a positive effect (e.g. Burić & Moè, 2020; Jungert, Levine & Koestner, 2020; Keller et al., 2016; Kim & Schallert, 2014). Seemingly it has to come from the heart. A final, recurring point in the evaluation was the appreciation of the transdisciplinary approach in which attention for addressing social justice topics and other present-day concerns (such as the invasion of Ukraine) was an integral part, as worded by one of the students:

> This course has been one of my favorites so far! When we started, I had very limited knowledge of Shakespeare and his plays, so when I'm reflecting on my evolution, I can definitely see that I've come a long way. What I enjoyed the most was the acting part because it allowed our creativity to flow and also we interacted a lot with each other during the preparation of the performances. Moreover, the fact that we studied Shakespeare's plays in connection to current issues was very insightful and eye-opening. Overall, I enjoyed the course a lot and I definitely encourage you to keep the same structure with the presentations and the actual performances. We all had a lot of fun! Finally, your humor and relaxed attitude were the cherries on the top of the cake! :)

The ambitious two-year course was an overwhelming success, and after the first two years, it has established itself as a standard part of the curriculum, with a new two-year course starting every year. Teaching transdisciplinary Shakespeare can be an incredibly rewarding and enjoyable privilege.

4.3.3 Compromises

In developing and teaching this course for the Honours College I had aimed at addressing some of my earlier concerns. The inclusion of two co-teachers in the Netherlands, one from the field of social sciences and one from the theatre industry, allowed for a more ambitious and diversified approach and also set my mind at rest about the adequacy of my grading. The wish to develop a course more specifically aimed at Shakespeare and social justice topics right from the start worked out well and aligned with the vision of the Honours College. And, finally, the 'real-life' experience I had aimed at was now an integral part of the course, not only in visiting four theatre productions and discussing them with academics and professionals in the summer school but also in writing, directing and performing a Shakespeare adaptation themselves. Building the course around four plays which we saw in the summer school also had its challenges: I could not start preparing the course and the assignments until some two weeks before the start of the course, while I also found myself 'at the mercy' of the theatre company's choices regarding their summer schedule. These were small hurdles, however: the first mainly required proper time management (and some busy evenings) before the start of the course while the repertoire of the two companies (over the past three years now) always provided enough material to work with in the context of transdisciplinary Shakespeare. The necessity to include a non-Shakespeare production in the first year of the course, which had irked me initially, proved to be a blessing in disguise and we have continued this tradition since. More serious challenges involved the workload and the length of the classes: scheduled between 19.00 and 21.00 in the evening (the normal time for an Honours class), they regularly ran over time by half an hour or even more, as in the one of the student comments:

> The time issue was a little bit problematic. In general I did not have problems with attending the class for three hours if it would have been communicated with us before. Maybe the teacher could 'warn' the following courses a little bit earlier that some sessions might take more time :)

This was a valid concern and caused in part by the enthusiasm of the students to engage in discussion and by my own reluctance to cut short these ongoing debates about Shakespeare's plays, characters, themes and social justice. While the course still tends to run over time occasionally, this is now generally limited to a quarter of an hour, half an hour at most and the students have received prior 'warnings'. The remarks about the workload in general ('Reading an entire play, analyzing a movie, and preparing for a presentation was often much work') were valid, but this was part and parcel of the idea of the pressure-cooker approach in the broadening module, although the planning and pre-required reading were improved in later years. All of the aforementioned concerns would have contributed to the relatively low score on the organisation of the course in the quantitative survey, which scored only a 3.4 as mentioned earlier. The changes I made in the next year seemingly had an effect as the grade improved to a 4.2 (still the lowest of the six questions, but now on a par with the score of the other Honours courses). Having found my feet in this transdisciplinary course to non-English literature students, a next step in the process towards transdisciplinary Shakespeare would be bringing these students from other disciplines and the traditional cohort of English literature students together in one course. To further complicate an already ambitious plan, this would take shape in the form of an international collaborative project between the University of Groningen and the University of Nottingham Trent, which I discuss in the next section.

5 Crossing Borders: International Transdisciplinarity

Faculties: University College Groningen (University of Groningen) & English Department (University of Nottingham Trent)

While the previous three courses were the result of initiative on my part, the most recent one was indirectly caused by an email of a fellow Shakespearean at Nottingham Trent University. A couple of months after the start of the Honours College course, this teacher contacted me to discuss a round table or a small online conference for students of ours which would focus on *The Merchant of Venice*, a play we had both published on. In the following months, I suggested we take it a step further and explore the possibility of a co-taught, partly online, class. These kinds of international projects are not uncommon in Shakespeare studies, as testified, for example, by a collaborative learning project between the University of Warwick, United Kingdom, and Monash University in Australia (Gregory, García Ochoa & Prescott, 2023). However, we aimed at taking it a step further and work across disciplines as well: English literature students at Nottingham Trent would cooperate with students of Social Sciences from the University College to explore the topic of the Other, using both *The Merchant of Venice* and *Othello* as the core plays. The reasons for choosing these two plays were partly practical: the two plays were already incorporated in the curriculum at Nottingham Trent and both the other teacher and I were very familiar with them, having published extensively on the topic of racial and ethnic representation in Shakespeare. The plays and their production histories and reception offered compelling case studies in the political and ideological concerns of the specific social and cultural fabrics of which they were a part in both Anglophone and non-Anglophone countries. In addition, students at the University College and the Honours College had earlier indicated their appreciation of addressing the topic of racial and ethnic injustice, also in light of the events following the murder of George Floyd in 2020 which accelerated worldwide interest in systemic racism and the histories and performances that perpetuate or challenge it.

Although my original idea had always been to reach out to non-English literature students on Shakespeare and social justice, this new cooperation did seem like a promising project from the perspective of transdisciplinary teaching. It would allow for a mixture of both groups: students of English literature (in Nottingham) would cooperate directly (online) with students from social sciences (in Groningen) on a topic with clear, topical, relevance. At the same time, I was slightly hesitant about the project. The idea of combining students from both disciplines in one course dedicated to Shakespeare and social justice was appealing, as was the idea of choosing the topic of the Other. However, starting a project along these lines with student groups who would physically be in different countries might complicate an already challenging course. As both of us had our hands full on the courses we were already running, we decided to integrate our project within existing courses. For this several hurdles had to be taken: the courses needed to take place at the same time, we would need approval from course coordinators and other staff on both sides and a budget might be useful as we wanted to include practitioners in the course and also teach each other's classes physically at least once.

Aligning the courses timewise, which Groningen would arrange, was a major hurdle as currently our courses were in different semesters. First, another course had to be found with the teacher agreeing to have it moved to my original semester. The organisation of this transfer of courses took a couple of months, which meant that the project would not start until the academic year 2022/2023. The approval by heads and directors was relatively straightforward in Groningen. In a conversation with the Director of Education, she had indicated that she was very happy about our plans overall and about the cooperation between Nottingham Trent University and the University of Groningen. In a follow-up session with the Academic Director of Humanities a final agreement was reached and the international collaboration between Trent and Groningen we aimed for was approved. For Nottingham Trent it took more than a couple of conversations, as an extensive proposal needed to be written, in part because they funded the additional costs of the proposed project, which became part of the so-called COIL trajectory (collaborative online international learning). The focus in the proposal would be on internationalisation and present-day relevance, which ticked the university's relevant boxes, as worded in the final version of the proposal:

> This interdisciplinary and cross-national course demonstrates the university's ability to discuss and analyse the intricate entanglements between the theatre and the world. Now, more than ever, deep cultural analysis across borders and disciplines is important for today's students, tomorrow's global citizens. (COIL, 2022)

A final hurdle for Nottingham was the necessity to change the assessment of the existing course. Previously this had been an essay, whereas now, at my behest, the assessment would be based on a group-based project (consisting of a total of five or six students per group, from both Nottingham and Groningen), which would discuss the topic of the Other as explored by *Othello* or *The Merchant of Venice*, and how these related to relevant challenges in today's society. They would present their findings in a joint online session (this could be in the format of a presentation or a more creative response, such as a short play, of fifteen to twenty minutes to be followed by an active discussion with the rest of the cohort (for which the presenters would be responsible) of approximately ten minutes. The proposed changes received their final approval and we were set to start. As the project would be incorporated on my end into the existing course 'Leadership in Culture', I altered the course guide and added that the topic of the Other would be explored and that one of the assignments would be taught and presented in cooperation with students from Nottingham Trent University. Of the eighteen (for Nottingham fourteen) regular lectures of the course, nine (for Nottingham six) would be dedicated to this specific transdisciplinary project, resulting in the following addition to the course description.

> International Project: This is a new element in the course, which constitutes a collaboration project with students of Nottingham Trent University. In groups comprising students from both universities, you prepare and deliver a presentation or AV production followed by a Q&A session. The focus is on 'the Other' and the impact of racial and ethnic differences. This could be a creative or critical response, developed in consultation with the other students in the group and supervised by tutors from Groningen and Nottingham Trent University.
>
> | | |
> |---|---|
> | *Hours per week* | 2 |
> | *Number of weeks* | 9 |
> | *Teaching method* | Seminar |
> | *Assessment* | Practical Group Project |
> | *Course type* | bachelor |
> | *Student composition* | Groningen: multidisciplinary (liberal arts and sciences) & international (25 per cent Dutch, 75 per cent international) |
> | | Nottingham: monodisciplinary (English) & largely UK |
> | *Number of instructors* | 4 (including 2 guest teachers) |
> | *ECTS* | 5 (for entire course) |

5.1 Course Set-Up and Lectures

In this section I will focus specifically on the nine lectures related to the cooperation between Groningen and Nottingham. Six of these lectures were joint, co-taught lectures taken by both groups simultaneously by way of a shared online platform. In order to determine the technical requirements of the online classroom and the continued functioning of the international student collaboration, we had a series of sessions with COIL and IT experts from both universities. First of all, we needed a shared educational software platform, which we did not yet have. For the duration of the course, Nottingham students, teachers and relevant IT staff would have guest access to Groningen's platform, Brightspace. By means of this shared platform we were able to communicate shared announcements and further content to all students, use the video classroom tool for sharing lectures, work with breakout rooms where necessary and generally enable students to cooperate online. In order to optimise the online classroom setting, we chose a system in which the Nottingham and Groningen students could see each other's classroom on a large screen, while the use of special microphones allowed for listening and talking to each other. What students particularly liked in this set-up was that it created for them a sense of a 'shared classroom' instead of the little stamp-like pictures of individual students which they were used to on platforms such as Zoom. In order to address any technical issues which might arise, IT specialists were in the classroom during the first sessions to assist. While we had, in theory at least, done our homework, covered the technical basics, consulted the experts and prepared for eventualities, reality proved more complicated. In the course of the lectures problems kept emerging in students failing to get access to Brightspace, video screens not working properly or sound issues as microphones worked perfectly during a test-run but then failed again a few minutes later. While it was fortunate that help was always close at hand, it did disrupt classes and kept causing unwanted delays.

In addition to the six mutual, co-taught lectures, I had included three additional lectures for my own students, whose knowledge of Shakespeare would be relatively limited compared to those of English literature students. These three lectures consisted of an initial exploration of *Othello* and *The*

Merchant of Venice, in order to bring them at least somewhat on a level with the Nottingham cohort. The first lecture took place two days before the introductory co-taught lecture of the COIL project and the other two lectures took each place two days before the co-taught COIL lectures on *The Merchant of Venice* and *Othello*. The first of these three lectures stuck to theory and was aimed at giving them a first sense of the potential relevance of the two plays as I had them choose and explore academic reviews of theatre productions, academic papers, book chapters or introductions of the two plays and indicate their relevance today (e.g. Apolloni, 2013; Bartelle, 2021; Heijes & Thompson, 2020; Heijes & Schülting, 2022; Kouts, 2018; Stein, 2005). Based on articles and book chapters from both Shakespeare, Jewish, leadership and psychoanalytic studies, it resulted in a broad discussion varying from 'interpersonal relationships on the socio-political, the organizational and the individual level', to the role of women, racism, anti-Semitism and 'the resurgence of anti-migrant or more broadly anti-other sentiments and issues of cultural identity, of cultural power struggles, and of xenophobia'. For the second and third lecture close reading, a further discussion on topicality and creative assignments were added and students would also watch the Laurence Fishburne *Othello* (Parker, 1995), the Al Pacino *Merchant* (Radford, 2004) and the stage-to-screen studio production of the National Theatre's *Merchant* directed by Trevor Nunn (2001), the latter also because it featured one of the guest teachers, Andrew French, as Launcelot Gobbo. This introduction to the two plays and their afterlives and relevance should provide the Dutch students with enough of a background to (hopefully) engage in a meaningful discussion with the guest teachers and the English literature cohort from Nottingham.

The aim of the first co-taught lecture in the 'shared classroom' was not only meant as an introduction to the project but also to get acquainted with the online platform Brightspace and the idea of a shared classroom and provide an opportunity for getting to know each other in the subgroups. We started off by introducing ourselves to the groups across borders and further explained the rationale behind COIL, the importance of international collaboration, transdisciplinarity and working with students from another discipline, the schedule of the project and the assessments. We next divided the group into five subgroups of six students, consisting of equally distributed students from Groningen and Nottingham and gave these groups two assignments to address in 'break-out rooms', which are online rooms in which students can, in subgroups, talk to and see each other. The idea behind it was to give them a sense of how Brightspace might work and to immediately establish communication between the members of the subgroups. We asked them (1) to discuss their expectations of COIL, group work and methods of communication between group members and (2) to consider whether '*Othello* [is] a racist play? Don't worry about agreeing in your groups but be prepared to discuss / present your findings to the whole cohort'. Afterwards the subgroups came back to the shared classroom and discussed their findings with the other groups. We had got off to a good start and the groups were up and running.

The second lecture would focus on '*Othello*, Race, Acting, Production and the Theatre Industry' and would require me to travel to Nottingham (as mentioned earlier, we would teach each other's classes physically once) to physically meet the students and give a lecture. The lecture would be streamed to the Groningen students to allow them to participate through the shared classroom and an assistant would be available in the Groningen classroom for any problems that might arise. By way of an interactive case study, we discussed *Othello* within the framework of racial discourse, national identity, cognitive dissonance, white fragility and uncomfortable truths. After the break Andrew French, one of the two guest teachers and a well-known actor, briefly discussed his experiences as an actor playing Launcelot Gobbo. Next, he extensively discussed his role as Othello, the play itself, – which he referred to as the O.J. Simpson story of all time –, its controversies and colour-blind versus colour-conscious casting. When time for questions came, they were mainly the Groningen students who engaged in a discussion and many of the questions were fairly direct and even personal:

- Do you invest your own self into the play?
- Does an all-black production of *Othello* make sense?
- Is racial injustice discussed during rehearsals with other actors or even in the theatre industry?
- Is it a painful play for you as a person?

During the Q&A session the Nottingham teacher advised Andrew French a couple of times that he did not need to answer these questions as they evidently touched upon possibly sensitive topics. Perhaps there is a cultural difference between addressing personal topics at English universities versus Dutch universities, or perhaps the Groningen students were just emboldened as I had encouraged them not to shy away from controversial questions. Whatever the reason, Andrew French was never deterred and answered all questions quite frankly, speaking about discrimination within the English theatre industry, about the conflict and the pain in playing Othello as an actor and how one got caught in one's own preconceptions, about stereotypical audience reactions and the lack of black actors in white roles. It was an impressive session and arguably one of the highlights of the course. It motivated one of the subgroups to actually take up the topic of colour and casting at the Royal Shakespeare Company for their final assignment.

The third lecture worked with the same format, only this time the Nottingham teacher came to Groningen to physically meet and teach the student group, with the Nottingham cohort being present through the shared classroom. This lecture focused on *The Merchant of Venice* and more in particular on the controversial nature of the play, the character of Shylock and its potential for anti-Semitism, while providing an overview of relevant theatre productions. The guest teacher for this session was Justus van Oel, a translator, actor and columnist who had adapted *The Merchant of Venice* and re-named it *The Arab of Amsterdam* (Oel, 2007). In the play Shylock was renamed Rafi, an Arab Jew who had migrated from Iraq to Amsterdam, where his outsider status had changed from a Jew in an Arab country to an Arab in the Netherlands. The play was staged three years after the assassination of Theo van Gogh – a director with whom Van Oel had closely cooperated – by a Dutch-Moroccan member of a fundamentalist Muslim network. Within an increasingly xenophobic context in the Netherlands, the production was well received as a timely and relevant denunciation of racism and a powerful plea for tolerance (Heijes, 2022: 184–185). Van Oel spoke with the students about the 'immeasurable fame of Shakespeare' that stands 'between him and his audience', arguing that

> the words of his characters have turned into memes, they are
> no longer the story of a person, not something that is felt,
> but something that is recognised. Ah! To be or not to be!
> I know that one. Mental selfie.

In his adaptations he aimed at 'freeing' Shakespeare and making him relevant for today's audiences and while Van Oel explained how he himself loved the sheer poetic beauty of his plays, he also attacked *The Merchant of Venice* for its potential for anti-Semitism. At the end of his adaptation, immediately after the trial scene, the character Shakespeare himself appeared on stage, dressed in close resemblance to the Cobbe portrait, and was derided by all other actors for creating such an easy vehicle for anti-Semitism: 'A Shylock such as this would sell like hot cakes, William, and you knew it.' It resulted in another lively discussion, this time on Shakespeare, *Merchant* and the need for adapting his plays. Our decision to include practitioners had turned out quite well as would also be confirmed later in the student evaluations.

The student groups had by now started working on their final products and while they had discussed their initial ideas already informally with us over the past few weeks, we had also scheduled one formal session to discuss and monitor their progress, after which they had another four to five weeks to prepare their presentation or production. In the end, three of the groups focused on *Othello* basing themselves on a variety of sources not only from Shakespeare studies, but also based on racial, historical and sociopolitical research (e.g. Brucher, 1994; Christofides, 2021; Laqueur, 1976; Lebron, 2017; Phipps, 2021; Thompson, 2021; Wekker, 2016). Two of these products were regular PowerPoint presentations discussing how companies had staged *Othello* in a variety of countries both before and after the rise of the BLM movement. They focused on costume, set and casting choices, audience reception, sociopolitical context and language in countries including South Africa, Germany, Poland, the Netherlands, the UK, Cyprus and the United States from the end of the twentieth century until very recently, including JaMeeka D. Holloway's 2021 Zoom production (due to Covid) for the Women's Theatre Festival and Clint Dyer's production which was still on at the National Theatre at the time of the presentation. It resulted in a discussion of the extent to which racial dynamics were underlying these production choices, how the play reflected wider cultural concerns and to what extent it might even act as an agent for change (or not). The third group chose a different approach and focused on audience reaction to productions of the play from the eighteenth to the twentieth centuries and did so by way of three imaginary conversations between audience members, acted out by students. These conversations were framed by timelines indicating audience attitudes and responses and social/political highlights of the period in question to give a general background context. The three imaginary conversations took place in respectively 1714 between a higher-class and a lower-class audience member, in 1833 (the year of the Abolition of Slavery Act in the UK) between an abolitionist and a pro-slavery journalist who had both attended an Ira Aldridge production, a small fragment of which is included as follows:

> Audience member 1: Amazing! I have never seen an *Othello* play as authentically as that. Finally someone who shares the same heritage plays the leading role.
> Audience member 2: Tsss. It was awful. To see a man like that touch that poor woman. He shouldn't even be on that stage, let alone as a Shakespearean hero like Othello.

The third conversation took place in 1964 in response to the Laurence Olivier performance of Othello at the National Theatre, which was also produced as a movie the year after. It was a creative and bold approach, not only based on reviews (generally lacking in 1714) but also on more general attitudes towards race and racism in the different timeframes. In their use of racial slurs in audience reactions, trying to mimic racist responses of earlier periods, the group mirrored practices in translations in non-Anglophone countries where offensive racial terms, including the N-word, are sometimes used by translators to stress and enhance the racism in the play. This led to a valuable conversation between UK and non-Anglophone students on the different historical and cultural sensitivities to the usage of these words not only as terms of abuse but also as instruments of enslavement.

The fourth presentation also chose a more creative approach and took the format of a pre-recorded Zoom-conference in which the student host discussed '*The Merchant of Venice*, a well-known Shakespeare play that has long been the subject of controversy, particularly regarding Jewish representation'. The host had invited two researchers, an actor, a producer, an audience member and a critic who engaged in a discussion about the play, its productions, the representation of Shylock and anti-Semitism through the centuries. The final and fifth group was inspired, as mentioned earlier, by the guest teacher Andrew French and they gave a PowerPoint presentation on 'Colour, Casting and the RSC', making critical use of good references to recent RSC productions of plays such as *Hamlet*, *Much Ado About Nothing* and *Romeo and Juliet*. It was a brave departure from the original texts which we had discussed in class, but it aligned well with the general theme of the course and its focus on the Other in Shakespeare, building on French's criticism of the theatre industry while also addressing to what extent casting choices of the RSC related more in general to British society and culture. As part of their research the students had also interviewed Jami Rogers, author of *British Black and Asian Shakespeareans* (2022) and the creator of the British Black and Asian Shakespeare Performance Database, about both the RSC and an ongoing trend 'of denying the significant and long-standing presence of non-Caucasians in British culture'. In the following discussion, it was argued by the student group that while some progress might have been made, 'the state of inclusivity at the RSC is not rosy to the point where it is that great of an example'.

5.2 Aftermath
5.2.1 Grading

Although I had not yet graded a collaborative transdisciplinary project across borders and between two student cohorts from different disciplines, my past experience in transdisciplinary Shakespeare combined with the views of my co-teachers in those courses had made me feel more comfortable in my grading skills of these type of courses. For this specific project, the grading process was performed by three persons: next to the two teachers of the course, Nottingham Trent University also had standard regulations in place that required that grades be ratified by a second internal marker. While not involved in the project itself, this second marker of

Nottingham Trent had attended the presentations of the final products and was also well versed in Shakespeare studies. As the groups consisted of a mix of Nottingham and Groningen students, we would need to reach agreement on the grades which was achieved fairly quickly in a three-person meeting. Just as in my previous courses, the grades for this course also averaged the high grade of an eight. The quality that students had achieved in previous courses on transdisciplinary Shakespeare in the Netherlands extended to my delight also to collaboration across borders between students from two different universities and faculties. There was a notable difference though between the relative weight of the grades. For Nottingham students the grade on their final project weighed for 80 per cent in their ultimate grade for the entire course, whereas for Groningen students it only weighed for 20 per cent in their final grade. Considering the time spent on the project by the students, neither of these percentages seemed a correct representation within the framework of the entire course of which the project was a part, so we would need to align this better in the future.

5.2.2 Student Evaluation

As in previous courses, the student evaluations were anonymous and both of us were highly curious about the final verdict of the students as this was our first time providing a cross-border course across disciplines, while for Nottingham students the type of creative assignment was a new element as well. During the course itself, students from both sides had already expressed concerns about the technical hiccups and one group in particular suffered from the fact that two out of three Nottingham students did not show up at any meetings at all in spite of repeated attempts at contact from their fellow students (and from us after we were informed). Even though these two students were ultimately removed from the course, it resulted in a poor start for this specific group. The evaluations on Nottingham side were both quantitative and qualitative, with a response score of circa 40 per cent, although the qualitative remarks were less extensive than on the Groningen side, possibly due to the fact that the Groningen students only provided a qualitative evaluation (roughly an A4 per student). The Nottingham scores on teaching and on organisation were both 4.1, the score on assessment and feedback was 3.8 and the overall satisfaction score was

3.6, resulting in average score of 3.9 for the course. As the student evaluations covered the entire course and not just the COIL project, the quantitative Nottingham evaluation was slightly less useful as it was unclear how heavy the COIL project weighed into this evaluation. The qualitative feedback threw some more light on the COIL project and asked about what went well, some brief student comments pointed out the 'collaborative communication with international students', the 'ability to work within a group and be creative', 'looking at modern adaptations', 'learning about colour casting' as well as 'looking at contemporary matters in relation to Shakespeare'. These brief comments aligned with the slightly more extensive comments of two students on the project:

> I really enjoyed working alongside a different university from a different country gaining perspective to the subject I otherwise wouldn't have had. I also enjoyed being able to have a meeting with an actor within the same sector.
> I really enjoyed the COIL section of this module as it was something different and enabled us more freedom in our final projects.

These comments were valuable, as interdisciplinarity and present-day relevance are cornerstones behind transdisciplinary Shakespeare and extending the collaboration even further across borders and bringing students of English literature and students from other disciplines together seemed to work well for the Nottingham group. In addition, the freedom in executing the final creative assignment was appreciated. It made a change from the traditional exams or essay-writing projects which they were more used to. Criticism on the course related in part to technical hurdles ('Everything worked well except for technical issues') and problems of communication across borders, although students tried ways to get around this:

> I liked the fact that it was a collaborative project, however it was often difficult trying to communicate back and forth with relatively quick responses with the Dutch students.

> Despite this challenge we made the best of it by getting in touch via Whatsapp and video calls through the weeks.

A very specific comment of a student was content-oriented and related to the two plays studied as the student would have preferred 'learning about Othello and Merchant of Venice before the COIL project'. In Groningen I had chosen to do so in three preparatory lectures to bring our students somewhat on a level with the Nottingham cohort, but possibly these type of lectures might also have been incorporated into the COIL project as a whole.

On the Groningen side the student response score was a hundred per cent and consisted of an extensive qualitative evaluation, allowing us to get a firm understanding of how students had experienced the collaborative project. Just as the Nottingham group, the students mentioned technical issues causing problems in online teaching and communication, while at the same time they highly valued working with students from another university and discipline, as exemplified in the following two reactions:

> The collaboration with the Trent University students was really fun and motivating. Their English language insights were interesting and worked quite well with the Shakespearean part of the course. Moreover, the link between Shakespeare and 21-st century challenges is the key to this project and where we and English literature students meet.
>
> I was strongly fascinated by their literary knowledge, specifically about Shakespeare. It was very interesting to be able to work with individuals that add such a new dimension and perspective to the assignments. The combination of structuring, creativity and social justice topics that we from Groningen had, in combination with their deep Shakespeare understanding allowed us to have a rich project.

However, when considering aspects such as work ethos and group participation in the evaluation, a different picture emerged, with some of the Groningen groups being critical of their Nottingham peers.

> Overall, I really enjoyed the project, but I was less impressed by the UK students. Perhaps this was my group in specific but I felt as if they didn't participate as much as the Groningen students did.
>
> Within my group, it seemed that most of the Nottingham participants were only looking to do the least amount of work possible.

Of the five groups, two did not experience this lack of commitment and in these groups cooperation worked out quite well from the start with students evaluating their UK peers in terms of students that were 'proactive'. Two other groups, which had started off poorly, did find their stride in the course of the project and indicated a change for the better in cooperation:

> However, once we found our groove and started having regular meetings, I think the UK students (that were left from our group) showed equal effort as we did. I enjoyed their inputs, thoughts, opinions and viewpoints and thought it was special to have a chance to work together with them.
>
> At first, it seemed their work ethics diverged from ours sometimes. Nonetheless, I like academic challenges and having to collaborate with others. As our group members got more familiar with each other we also developed some strong ideas and were very satisfied with our interaction.

A fifth group had a total lack of participation from two Nottingham students, as mentioned earlier, which ultimately led to them being removed from the course. Although this resulted in a poor start, the remaining Nottingham student was a breath of much needed fresh air for the Groningen cohort:

> Regardless, there was also one Nottingham student that was very active and had a lot of very interesting and helpful inputs. It was extremely nice to work with her and she had a high understanding of the texts we were discussing. Working with her was not only productive, but something to look forward to.

In the end, all groups, each in their own way, managed to address the challenges involved in working with students whose work ethos seemed, at least in part, to be different from what they were used to. Whether it was just bad luck, whether Groningen students were simply more used to collaborative project work or whether it was caused by deeper, cultural differences between academic institutions or students was impossible to determine; the sample size was not large enough for that. It was, however, something which we would have to address and monitor more closely in later cross-border courses.

5.2.3 Compromises

In this course we had aimed at taking transdisciplinary Shakespeare a step further by bringing English literature students and students from other disciplines together in one course in the form of an international collaborative project between the Universities of Groningen and Nottingham Trent, focusing on the topic of the Other in Shakespeare and present-day society. Although the mutual visits of the teachers to each other's classes, the concept of a 'shared classroom' and granting access to the same educational online platform to all students provided a sense of direct communication, (minor) technical difficulties kept recurring in communication during lectures. Also, while we had managed to get the timetables in sync, differences in exam periods and vacation times resulted in planning difficulties for students. A major compromise we had to make, partly due to our own busy teaching schedules, was our decision to incorporate the project into an existing course of which it formed only a part, even if it was a significant part. While not directly caused by it, several of the course's concerns in the evaluations were arguably exacerbated by this compromise decision.

The project was to a certain extent comparable to the earlier mentioned (Section 1) collaboration between Warwick and Monash University (Gregory, García Ochoa & Prescott, 2023): working with a shared syllabus across national borders, including a creative project, employing the concept of a 'shared classroom' and also experiencing the seemingly inevitable technical difficulties. The focus in the Warwick-Monash cooperation highlighted the impact of the differences in cultural context. In our collaboration we took it a step further, both by physically teaching each other's student groups and by taking a more transdisciplinary approach: the main focus was an exploration of 'the Other' integrating the perspective of English Literature students (Nottingham) and those of Social Sciences students (the Netherlands) in subgroups evenly composed of both cohorts. The project was considered a success at Nottingham Trent University by higher management and the Head of English deemed the project an 'important initiative for both the department and the school' and indicated he was 'very keen to continue to support this project'. Likewise, the director of Nottingham Trent University Global argued it would be 'fantastic' if the project could be repeated next year. The Nottingham teacher was interviewed to discuss the success of the project, which became one of the University's four showcase COIL projects. At the same time, the project was effectively cancelled as Nottingham unexpectedly moved the module into the second half of the year, meaning that the timetables of the two courses in Groningen and Nottingham were once again out of sync.

The unexpected termination goes to demonstrate the (bureaucratic) vulnerability of these collaborative projects, no matter their seeming success. Irrespective of Nottingham's unexpected timetable changes, my hesitations at the start of the course had not proved to be entirely unfounded. On the one hand, the idea of these two student cohorts participating and learning from each other within the framework of social justice and Shakespeare seemed sound and did provide some good results and enthusiasm among the students. However, the technical issues, the differences in preparation and work ethos, exacerbated by the inability to have real-life sessions between students and the course being a project rather than a separate module, needed to be sorted out. Perhaps we had aimed too high and our project was possibly too much, too quick, too challenging. Amidst all of these concerns and compromises, the students highly appreciated the interdisciplinarity and topicality of the project and enjoyed the course and the creative assignments as exemplified by recurring adjectives in the evaluations such as 'enriching', 'enjoyable', 'exciting', 'motivating', 'refreshing' or 'engaging' with students recommending the course to their fellow students. It was perhaps best summarised by a student's one-liner in the evaluation: 'This is the one class I am looking so very, very much forward to each and every week.' No matter the compromises, no matter the difficulties, no matter the inexplicable bureaucratic wheels, in the end, this is what truly motivates me as a teacher.

6 Conclusion

Transdisciplinary Shakespeare Pedagogy offers a sense both of the opportunities and of the difficulties in teaching Shakespeare beyond the confines of the English literature department and provides possible ways forward on the road to wider cooperation, collaboration and integration between curriculums, teachers and students of different disciplines. This Element is based on four case studies of university courses, in which Shakespeare studies, social sciences and societal challenges are integrated and taught to a variety of students from different disciplines and countries. I discussed how we structured the courses, which type of students (faculties, year-levels, nationalities) we worked with, which plays, productions and social justice topics we addressed and what type of assignments we worked with, the compromises I had to make, the students' evaluations of the courses and the cooperation with other teachers, finding the balance between Shakespeare and present-day issues, how courses came into being and which hurdles I had to take not only in developing and teaching the courses but also in getting them approved in the first place. Starting out tentatively and under the umbrella of standard bachelor and master's theses at the Faculty of Economics and Business, I was surprised by the (unexpected) success of the courses and the appreciation not only by students but also by co-assessors at the faculty who even evaluated the final products higher than I did. Out of these first, tentative and somewhat uncertain steps, the courses gradually widened out to other faculties and became increasingly complex, hand in hand with my own growing experience. Starting out with a monodisciplinary group of Dutch students under a standardised format and focused on leadership and Shakespeare, later developed courses at other faculties started to include students (and teachers) from many different disciplines and countries and were hand-tailored to include a variety of social (in)justice topics in relation to Shakespeare. While this chronological throughline of increasing complexity may appear to be a linear process, and while inevitably my own experience grew as the courses developed alongside it, in reality the process of transdisciplinary Shakespeare was far from linear and on the way unexpected hurdles kept appearing over and over again.

In this Element I base myself on case study research – not uncommon in most research on Shakespeare pedagogy – as a particularly useful methodology when observation, detailed description, complexity and contextuality are of importance. However, case study research also has its limitations, a major one of which is generalizability. In order to address this, four different case studies have been included, comprising two different universities, two countries, four different faculties and a broad variety of students and teachers. Nevertheless, in the end, it remains a limited sample and each university and country has its own specific approaches, its own dilemmas, its own peculiarities, its own bureaucratic hurdles. However, the movement towards transdisciplinary Shakespeare builds on a wider trend in academia towards convergence in research and teaching in which crossing disciplinary boundaries and addressing current, societal challenges are central elements. The first of the four cornerstones of the strategic plan 2021–2026 of the University of Groningen refers directly to these two aspects, arguing that the university aims

> to stimulate learning and research in an interdisciplinary
> setting with and for regional, European and global partners
> to find sustainable, innovative solutions to the challenges
> that society faces. (University, 2021: 3)

The two terms in the title of the strategic plan, 'Connecting for Impact' succinctly incorporate these two elements, and they are terms that keep appearing in strategic plans at many other universities across the world. As such this Element is part of a wider movement, and hopefully these four case studies may provide further ideas and inspiration in teaching across disciplines via institutionally built curriculum structures.

In the process of writing *Transdisciplinary Shakespeare Pedagogy*, a situation arose at a UK university which is, unfortunately, exemplary for the situation at many universities, both in the UK and in other countries. The university in question was seen to be 'restructuring' Arts & Humanities with a cut in staffing of almost 50 per cent taking effect on 1 September 2024, with a further round of cuts planned for twelve months later. Arguably in order to prevent unwanted public exposure in newspapers, it would take effect through early retirement schemes and remaining staff going fractional so that compulsory redundancies could be avoided. They may be the 'horror stories of our times', in the words of a sympathetic colleague, but they are the reality we are faced with. The safe havens of English literature departments, let alone specialised Shakespeare sections, seem to be disappearing almost as rapidly as the coral reefs around the world. While I might wish it were different, they are occurrences such as the aforementioned which have been one of the reasons for my own ventures into transdisciplinary Shakespeare and wanting to explore different paths we might take in reaching out to other students and other faculties. It is not a panacea, it is not a Renaissance of Shakespeare studies, it is far from an easy path, it is also a path still rarely trodden and it takes a lot of energy, but it might be one of the possible ways not only to work on what we care about most, but also to engage with many more students than before.

In research on Shakespeare pedagogy, the societal impact of Shakespeare has become increasingly prominent and the general editors of the *Cambridge Elements Shakespeare and Pedagogy* series refer to this at the start of the video interview on the series website:

> Shakespeare is going through a very exciting moment at this time where we're bringing to bear on Shakespeare numerous contemporary issues and topics that we find particularly significant. They might be to do with race or gender and identity or eco-criticism and the climate, a whole range of different topics which are coming to bear on Shakespeare. (Semler, 2020: 0.54–1.20)

Present-day relevance, social justice and calls for collaboration and reaching across boundaries not only permeate most current studies on Shakespeare and pedagogy but also find their way into Shakespeare studies in general, conferences, special issues, articles and books which highlight the deep entanglement between Shakespeare and social (in)justice. At the same time, research on transdisciplinary Shakespeare and structurally bridging across disciplines within institutional contexts is still few and far between. In *Transdisciplinary Shakespeare Pedagogy* I have aimed at providing a detailed analysis of crossing boundaries between disciplines and faculties within universities. Reaching out to other students connects not only with the increased interest of Shakespeare scholars or the strategic plans of universities but also with the interests of students who have shown themselves, in all case studies, to be eager to cross disciplinary boundaries and engage with relevant topics and challenges that confront them in today's societies. Transdisciplinary Shakespeare may well be a relatively new and hopefully inspiring element both in our teaching and in our research as increased collaboration, for example, with colleagues from the field of social sciences, might connect us with a range of other scholarship and help open up a broader spectrum of academic publication options. There is a world out there waiting to be explored perhaps more than we have done so far.

At the same time, it is also necessary to be aware of the challenges, compromises and even frustrations that one may encounter in reaching out to students beyond our traditional cohort and setting up structurally transdisciplinary courses across institutional boundaries. While universities may share strategic similarities, operationalising these strategies into concrete teaching practices and actually crossing the boundaries between faculties is inevitably fraught with local obstacles and in the process of introducing new courses, starting collaborative projects or crossing disciplines one will inevitably be confronted with specific and often differing budget systems, disciplinary walls, rigid bureaucracies or vested interests that may be frustrating at times. Semler, Hansen and Manuel rightfully speak of the 'pointless administrative churn and managerial interference' that confront teachers in innovative projects (2023: 10) as happened, for example, in the cross-border collaboration in the final case study, irrespective of the high praise it received. However, each university also has its own loopholes, its own 'chink in the wall', its own enthusiastic and supportive decision-makers, and one needs to be pro-active in finding these chinks, these centres of possible interest in exploring new territory. In this Element, I have aimed at describing the challenges in developing and getting courses accepted, but there is no one right way, as these four case studies show. Sometimes a mere suggestion is enough, as in the first case study, sometimes one needs political manoeuvring, as in the case of the University College, and sometimes one just needs a bit of luck, as in the case of the Honours College where a blog of the Dean appeared at just the right moment.

Not only the introduction of new courses, but also the teaching itself to a wide array of students from different disciplines is fraught with inevitable challenges, and many of these I have discussed in this Element, such as getting the students on the same level, finding a balance between Shakespeare and societal challenges, starting out relatively simple, collaborating with colleagues from other disciplines and, perhaps above all, providing a safe teaching environment as many of these students are asked to engage in new territory and move outside of their comfort zone. They are, however, not only students but also we, teachers, who venture beyond our traditional students and subjects and immediate expertise. Being aware of one's own limitations as a teacher is an important part of transdisciplinary Shakespeare: even though I possess the luxury of a multidisciplinary background myself, in the course of further refining these courses I have found it to be highly beneficial to include teachers from other disciplines as well. Over the course of teaching transdisciplinary Shakespeare I have been working with psychology, business, philosophy, European culture, communication, political science, gender studies, law, international relations, medical humanities and many other students from all over the world. While we have encountered several challenges varying from scheduling issues, lack of clarity, technical hiccups, collaboration across borders, time management, workload or budgetary constraints, these never seemed to have deterred the drive and enthusiasm of the students. The evaluations and perhaps above all the interest in not only a transdisciplinary approach to societal challenges but also in literature in general and the plays and productions of Shakespeare in particular have far exceeded my expectations. Throughout *Transdisciplinary Shakespeare Pedagogy* I have included responses, evaluations and comments from these students, and I think it no more than fitting to round off this Element with a citation from one of the student evaluation forms. It is, after all, for them that we are doing what we do: teach.

> One thing that stood out to me was how my perception of
> art changed during the course, or simply creating things out

of creativity. Shakespeare managed to provoke such intense discussions and nuanced perspectives within the span of about two months within our classroom and the information one can extract from analysing Shakespeare seems boundless. This made me create a more genuine appreciation for really all forms of art. I'm not entirely sure if this sort of epiphany I had came strictly from this course or just general growth and other external stimuli, but what definitely contributed to this is Coen's passion for Shakespeare and being a lecturer. I could not understand the relevance of literature or art, but because he always seemed so excited to teach us his insights, I felt morally inclined to give Shakespeare a chance, and definitely learned a new way of thinking regarding art, so-called objective truth, and how to extract information from new sources of information (like Shakespeare's plays). [. . . .] In conclusion, I highly recommend this course, which focused on contemporary issues related to Shakespeare and his plays. Although it was challenging at times, it provided a unique and creative learning experience compared to other courses offered at UCG. Shakespeare once wrote 'Nothing will come of nothing'. After this course I am sure about one thing; much can come from much, and much we got during this course.

References

Apolloni, Jessica (2013). 'Shylock Meets Palestine: Rethinking Shakespeare in Abdelkader Benali's Yasser', *Shakespeare Bulletin*, 31(2): 213–232.

Appignanesi, Richard & Robert Deas (2008). *Manga Shakespeare: Macbeth*. New York: Amulet Books.

Bachelor's Thesis Economics & Business University of Groningen (2018). https://ocasys.rug.nl/2018-2019/catalog/course/EBB731B10?legacy=true. Last accessed on 18 October 2024.

Baldwin, James (1964). 'Why I Stopped Hating Shakespeare,' in Randall Kenan, ed., *The Cross of Redemption: Uncollected Writings* (2010), New York: Pantheon, 53–56.

Bartelle, Michael Joel (2021). 'Review of Shakespeare's Othello (directed by Iqbal Khan for the Royal Shakespeare Company)', *Shakespeare*, 17(1): 83–87.

Bates, Laura (2013). *Shakespeare Saved My Life: Ten Years in Solitary with the Bard*. Naperville, IL: Sourcebooks.

Bernstein, Jay Hillel (2015). 'Transdisciplinarity: A Review of Its Origins, Development, and Current Issues', *Journal of Research Practice*, 11(1): 1–20.

Bickley, Pamela & Jenny Stevens, eds. (2023). *Shakespeare, Education and Pedagogy: Representations, Interactions and Adaptations*. London: Routledge.

Boublil, Alain & Claude-Michel Schönberg (1980). *Les Misérables* [Musical]. Paris: Palais des Sports, directed by Robert Houssein.

Branagh, Kenneth (1989). *Henry V* [Film]. London: BBC Film.

Branagh, Kenneth (1993). *Much Ado about Nothing* [Film]. Hollywood, FL: Samuel Goldwyn.

British Shakespeare Association (2021). *Online Conference CfP. Shakespeare In/Action*. https://memorients.com/events/online-conference%2Fcfp-shakespeare-in%2Faction. Last accessed on 18 October 2024.

Brucher, Richard (1994). 'O'Neill, Othello and Robeson', *The Eugene O'Neill Review*, 18(1/2): 45–58.

Burić, Irena & Angelica Moè (2020). 'What Makes Teachers Enthusiastic: The Interplay of Positive Affect, Self-Efficacy and Job Satisfaction', *Teaching and Teacher Education*, 89: 1–10.

Carbone, Courtney (2016). *OMG Shakespeare: Macbeth #killingit*. New York: Penguin Random House.

Cavanagh, Sheila & Steve Rowland (2023). 'Shakespeare in and out of Prison: A Collaboration between the World Shakespeare Project and Shakespeare Central', in Liam E. Semler, Claire Hansen & Jacqueline Manuel, eds., *Reimagining Shakespeare Education: Teaching and Learning through Collaboration*. Cambridge: Cambridge University Press, 127–138.

Christofides, Roger M. (2021). 'Hamlet versus Othello: Or, Why the White Boy Keeps Winning', *Shakespeare*, 17(1): 6–14.

Ciulla, Joanne B. (2019). 'The Two Cultures: The Place of Humanities Research in Leadership Studies', *Leadership*, 15(4): 433–444.

COIL (2022). *Coil Proposal: The 'Other' in Shakespeare: Contemporary Representations of Racial Difference in England and the Netherlands*. [unpublished document].

Crash Course Videos (2011 and following). www.youtube.com/watch?v=Sc850jqMcwo. Last accessed on 18 October 2024.

Crowe, Heljä Antola, Kendra Brandes, Beto Davison Aviles, Deborah Erickson & Dawn Hall (2013). 'Transdisciplinary Teaching: Professionalism across Cultures', *International Journal of Humanities and Social Sciences*, 3(13): 194–205.

Dadabhoy, Ambereen & Nedda Mehdizadeh (2023). *Anti-Racist Shakespeare*. Cambridge: Cambridge University Press.

Davies, Mary (2023). '"Radical Mischief": The Other Place Collaboration between the Royal Shakespeare Company and the University of Birmingham', in Liam E. Semler, Claire Hansen & Jacqueline Manuel, eds., *Reimagining Shakespeare Education: Teaching and Learning through Collaboration*. Cambridge: Cambridge University Press, 87–101.

Deckers, Jan (2021). 'The Value of Autoethnography in Leadership Studies, and Its Pitfalls', *Philosophy of Management*, 20: 75–91.

Della Gatta, Carla (2019). 'Confronting Bias and Identifying Facts: Teaching Resistance through Shakespeare', in Hillary Eklund & Wendy Beth Hyman, eds., *Teaching Social Justice through Shakespeare: Why Renaissance Literature Matters Now*. Edinburgh: Edinburgh University Press, 165–173.

Demeter, Jason M. (2019). 'African-American Shakespeares: Loving Blackness as Political Resistance', in Hillary Eklund & Wendy Beth Hyman, eds., *Teaching Social Justice through Shakespeare: Why Renaissance Literature Matters Now*. Edinburgh: Edinburgh University Press, 67–75.

Desai, Adhaar Noor (2019). 'Topical Shakespeare and the Urgency of Ambiguity', in Hillary Eklund & Wendy Beth Hyman, eds., *Teaching Social Justice through Shakespeare: Why Renaissance Literature Matters Now*. Edinburgh: Edinburgh University Press, 27–35.

Donaldson, Peter S. (1991). 'Taking on Shakespeare: Kenneth Branagh's *Henry V*', *Shakespeare Quarterly*, 42(1): 60–71.

Doran, Gregory, dir. (2015). *Henry V*. Performed Stratford-upon-Avon, Royal Shakespeare Theatre: Royal Shakespeare.

Egan, Michael (2000). 'Managers as Kings: Shakespeare on Modern Leadership', *Management Decision*, 38(5), 315–327.

Eklund, Hillary & Wendy Beth Hyman (2019). *Teaching Social Justice through Shakespeare: Why Renaissance Literature Matters Now*. Edinburgh: Edinburgh University Press.

Elzinga, Hanny (2014). *Een Wijde Blik Verruimt het Denken: A Broad View Expands the Mind*. Groningen: Rijksuniversiteit Groningen.

Elzinga, Hanny (2020). 'Pass the Strategy Blog – Hanny Elzinga', *Infonet*, University of Groningen. https://myuniversity.rug.nl/

infonet/medewerkers/actueel/news/pass-the-strategy-blog-hanny-elzinga. Last accessed on 18 October 2024.

Etzold, Veit (2012). 'Power Plays: What Shakespeare Can Teach on Leadership', *Business Strategy Series*, 13(2), 63–69.

Faculty of Economics and Business, University of Groningen (2016). *Strategic Plan 2016–2020*. www.rug.nl/feb/organization/feb-strategic-plan-2016-2020.pdf. Last accessed on 18 October 2024.

Faculty of Economics and Business, University of Groningen (2021). *Vision on Teaching and Learning FEB*. www.rug.nl/feb/organization/mission-vision-values/strategic-plan-2021-2026.pdf. Last accessed on 18 October 2024.

Flavian, Heidi (2024). *Transdisciplinary Perspectives in Educational Research, Volume 8. Transdisciplinary Teaching in Inclusive Schools*. Cham: Springer International.

Flick, Uwe (2019). *An Introduction to Qualitative Research*. 6th Ed. Thousand Oaks, CA: Sage.

Freeman, Tierra M., Lynley H. Anderman & Jane M. Jensen (2007). 'Sense of Belonging in College Freshmen at the Classroom and Campus Levels', *The Journal of Experimental Education*, 75(3), 203–220.

Garcia, Venessa (2012). 'Constructing and Reconstructing Female Sexual Assault Victims within the Media', in Denise L. Bissler & Joan L. Conners, eds., *The Harms of Crime Media: Essays on the Perpetuation of Racism, Sexism and Class Stereotypes*. Jefferson, IA: Mcfarland, 18–38.

Gilman, Sander L., Helen King, Roy Porter, George S. Rousseau & Elaine Showalter (1993). *Hysteria beyond Freud*. Berkeley, CA: University of California Press.

Green, William David (2023). 'Review of William Shakespeare's *All's Well That Ends Well* (Directed by Blanche McIntyre for the Royal Shakespeare Company) at the Royal Shakespeare Theatre, Stratford-upon-Avon, 31 August 2022', *Shakespeare*, 19(3): 389–392.

Greenblatt, Stephen (2018). *Tyrant: Shakespeare on Power*. London: Penguin

Greenhalgh, Susanne (2024). 'Performance Review: All's Well That Ends Well by Blanche McIntyre, Todd MacDonald, Hayley Pepler, and John Wyver', *Cahiers Élisabéthains*, 113(1): 125–130.

Gregory, Fiona, Gabriel García Ochoa & Paul Prescott (2023). 'The Warwick-Monash Co-teaching Initiative: Shakespeare and Portal Pedagogy', in Liam E. Semler, Claire Hansen & Jacqueline Manuel, eds., *Reimagining Shakespeare Education: Teaching and Learning through Collaboration*. Cambridge: Cambridge University Press, 113–126.

Guskey, Thomas R. & Susan M. Brookhart, eds. (2019). *What We Know about Grading: What Works, What Doesn't, and What's Next*. Alexandria, VA: Association for Supervision & Curriculum Development.

Guyotte, Kelly W., Nicki W. Sochaka, Tracie E. Costantino, Joachim Walther & Nadia N. Kellam (2014). 'STEAM as Social Practice: Cultivating Creativity in Transdisciplinary Spaces', *Art Education*, 67(6): 12–19.

Hahn, Louisa (2023). 'What Can Hamlet Teach Us about Queerness?' in Pamela Bickley & Jenny Stevens, eds., *Shakespeare, Education and Pedagogy: Representations, Interactions and Adaptations*. London: Routledge, 154–162.

Hansen, Claire (2023). 'Shakespeare, Climate Change and the Blue Humanities: Imagining an Oceanic Education', in Pamela Bickley & Jenny Stevens, eds., *Shakespeare, Education and Pedagogy: Representations, Interactions and Adaptations*. London: Routledge, 190–199.

Harris, Juliette & Toni Wynn (2012). 'Toward a STEM + Arts Curriculum: Creating the Teacher Team', in *Art Education*, 65(5): 42–47.

Heijes, Coen (2020). *Shakespeare, Blackface and Race: Different Perspectives*. Cambridge: Cambridge University Press.

Heijes, Coen (2022). 'Dutch Negotiations with Otherness in Times of Crisis', in Boika Sokolova & Janice Valls-Russell, eds., *Shakespeare's*

Others in 21st-Century European Performance: The Merchant of Venice and Othello. London: The Arden Shakespeare, 171–189.

Heijes, Coen & Ayanna Thompson (2020). 'Introduction: Shakespeare, Blackface and Performance: A Global Perspective', *Multicultural Shakespeare: Translation, Appropriation and Performance*, 22: 9–16.

Heijes, Coen & Sabine Schülting (2022). 'Introduction: Shakespeare and the Jews', *Shakespeare*, 18(1): 1–7.

Hennessey, Katherine (2023). 'Shakespeare, University Education, and Anti-Racism in Kuwait: "A Drop of Water in the Breaking Gulf"', in Pamela Bickley & Jenny Stevens, eds., *Shakespeare, Education and Pedagogy: Representations, Interactions and Adaptations*. London: Routledge, 172–180.

Hennink, Monique, Inge Hutter & Ajay Bailey (2020). *Qualitative Research Methods*. Los Angeles, CA: Sage.

Herbel Jr., Jerry E. (2015). 'Shakespeare's Machiavellian Moment: Discovering Ethics and Forming a Leadership Narrative in *Henry V*', *Public Integrity*, 17(3), 265–278.

Hobgood, Alison P. (2019). 'Shakespeare in Japan: Disability and a Pedagogy of Disorientation', in Hillary Eklund & Wendy Beth Hyman, eds., *Teaching Social Justice through Shakespeare: Why Renaissance Literature Matters Now*. Edinburgh: Edinburgh University Press, 46–54.

Holley, Lynn C. & Sue Steiner (2005). 'Safe Spaces: Student Perspectives on Classroom Environment', *Journal of Social Work Education*, 41(1): 49–64.

Honours College (2023). *Bachelor's Honours Programme*. www.rug.nl/education/honours-college/. Last accessed on 18 October 2024.

House, Robert J., Paul J. Hanges, Mansour Javidan, Peter W. Dorfman & Vipin Gupta, eds. (2004). *Culture, Leadership, and Organizations: The GLOBE Study of 62 Societies*. Thousand Oaks, CA: Sage.

Interagency Working Group on Convergence (2022). *Convergence Education: A Guide to Transdisciplinary Stem Learning and Teaching*. www.white

house.gov/wp-content/uploads/2022/11/Convergence_Public-Report_Final.pdf. Last accessed 18 October 2024.

Johanson, Kristine (2023). 'Co-opting "the Bard" as Manager in the Anglophone World and the Netherlands: Shakespeare for Synergy?' in Pamela Bickley & Jenny Stevens, eds., *Shakespeare, Education and Pedagogy: Representations, Interactions and Adaptations*. London: Routledge, 181–189.

Jones, Emily Griffith (2019). 'Global Performance and Local Reception: Teaching Hamlet and More in Singapore', in Hillary Eklund & Wendy Beth Hyman, eds., *Teaching Social Justice through Shakespeare: Why Renaissance Literature Matters Now*. Edinburgh: Edinburgh University Press, 55–63.

Josephine, Charlie (2022). *I, Joan*. London: Samuel French.

Jungert, Thomas, Shelby Levine & Richard Koestner (2020). 'Examining How Parent and Teacher Enthusiasm Influences Motivation and Achievement in STEM', *The Journal of Educational Research*, 113(4): 275–282.

Karim-Cooper, Farah (2021). 'Shakespeare through Decolonization', *English: Journal of the English Association*, 70(271): 319–324.

Karim-Cooper, Farah, Gordon McMullan, Lucy Munro & Will Tosh (2023). 'The Shakespeare's Globe/King's College London MA Shakespeare Studies: The First Twenty Years of Collaboration', in Liam E. Semler, Claire Hansen & Jacqueline Manuel, eds., *Reimagining Shakespeare Education: Teaching and Learning through Collaboration*. Cambridge: Cambridge University Press, 102–112.

Keller, Melanie M., Anita Woolfolk Hoy, Thomas Goetz & Anne C. Frenzel (2016). 'Teacher Enthusiasm: Reviewing and Redefining a Complex Construct', *Educational Psychology Review*, 28(4): 743–769.

Kemp, Sawyer (2019). 'Shakespeare in Transition: Pedagogies of Transgender Justice and Performance', in Hillary Eklund & Wendy

Beth Hyman, eds., *Teaching Social Justice through Shakespeare: Why Renaissance Literature Matters Now*. Edinburgh: Edinburgh University Press, 36–45.

Kim, Taehee & Diane L. Schallert (2014). 'Mediating Effects of Teacher Enthusiasm and Peer Enthusiasm on Students' Interest in the College Classroom', *Contemporary Educational Psychology*, 39(2): 134–144.

Kirwan, Peter (2023). 'All's Well That Ends Well (RSC) @ The Royal Shakespeare Theatre (film version)', *The Bardathon*. https://drpeterkirwan.com/2023/06/15/alls-well-that-ends-well-rsc-the-royal-shakespeare-theatre-film-version/. Last accessed on 18 October 2024.

Kouts, Gideon (2018). 'The Merchant of Venice in the Hebrew Press', *European Judaism: A Journal for the New Europe*, 51(2): 106–115.

Kurosawa, Akira (1957). *Throne of Blood* [Film]. Tokyo: Toho.

Laqueur, Thomas (1976). 'The Cultural Origins of Popular Literacy in England 1500–1850', *Oxford Review of Education*, 2(3): 255–275.

Leavy, Patricia (2011). *Essentials of Transdisciplinary Research: Using Problem-Centered Methodologies*. Walnut Creek, CA: Left Coast Press.

Lebron, Christopher J. (2017). *The Making of Black Lives Matter: A Brief History of an Idea*. New York: Oxford University Press.

Leon, Kenny, dir. (2019). *Much Ado about Nothing*. Performed New York, The Delacorte Theater: The Public Theater.

Leroy, Hannes, Michael E. Palanski & Tony Simons (2012). 'Authentic Leadership and Behavioral Integrity as Drivers of Follower Commitment and Performance', *Journal of Business Ethics*, 107(3), 255–264.

Ly, Ladj (2019). *Les Misérables* [Film]. Paris: SRAB Films.

Mackenzie, Rowan (2023). *Creating Space for Shakespeare: Working with Marginalized Communities*. London: The Arden Shakespeare.

Master's Thesis Economics & Business University of Groningen (2019). https://ocasys.rug.nl/2019-2020/catalog/course/EBM859B20. Last accessed on 18 October 2024.

McNamara, Leanna (2016). 'Hippocratic and Non-Hippocratic Approaches to Lovesickness', in Lesley Dean-Jones & Ralph Mark Rosen, eds., *Ancient Concepts of the Hippocratic: Studies in Ancient Medicine Series*, 46. Leiden: Brill, 308–327.

Mendoza, Kirsten N. (2019). 'Sexual Violence, Trigger Warnings, and the Early Modern Classroom', in Hillary Eklund & Wendy Beth Hyman, eds., *Teaching Social Justice through Shakespeare: Why Renaissance Literature Matters Now*. Edinburgh: Edinburgh University Press, 97–105.

Mentz, Steve (2019). 'Failing with Shakespeare: Political Pedagogy in Trump's America', in Hillary Eklund & Wendy Beth Hyman, eds., *Teaching Social Justice through Shakespeare: Why Renaissance Literature Matters Now*. Edinburgh: Edinburgh University Press, 134–141.

Morden, Tony (1997). 'Leadership as Competence', *Management Decision*, 35(7): 519–526.

Neely, Carol Thomas (2018). *Distracted Subjects: Madness and Gender in Shakespeare and Early Modern Culture*. Ithaca: Cornell University Press.

Neely, Adrian N., Asia S. Ivey, Catherine Duarte, Jocelyn Poe & Sireen Irsheid (2020). 'Building the Transdisciplinary Resistance Collective for Research and Policy: Implications for Dismantling Structural Racism as a Determinant of Health Inequity', *Ethnicity & Disease*, 30(3): 381–388.

Nunn, Trevor (2001). *The Merchant of Venice* [Film]. London: Lexington Road Entertainment Group.

Nussbaum, Martha C. (2017). *Not for Profit: Why Democracy Needs the Humanities – Updated Edition*. Princeton, TX: Princeton University Press.

O'Brien, Molly Townes, Tania Leiman & James Duffy (2014). 'The Power of Naming: The Multifaceted value of Learning Students' Names', *QUT Law Review*, 14(1): 114–128.

Oel, Justus van (2007). *De Arabier van Amsterdam* [*The Arab of Amsterdam*]. Amsterdam: DNA.

Olivier, Larence (1944). *Henry V* [Film]. London: Eagle-Lion Distributors.

Olivier, Richard (2013). *Inspirational Leadership: Timeless Lessons for Leaders from Shakespeare's Henry V*. London. England: Nicholas Brealey.

Osborne, Jeffrey (2019). 'Rural Shakespeare and the Tragedy of Education', in Hillary Eklund & Wendy Beth Hyman, eds., *Teaching Social Justice through Shakespeare: Why Renaissance Literature Matters Now*. Edinburgh: Edinburgh University Press, 107–114.

Palfrey, John (2017). *Safe Spaces, Brave Spaces: Diversity and Free Expression in Education*. Cambridge, MA: The MIT Press.

Panjwani, Varsha (2022). *Podcasts and Feminist Shakespeare Pedagogy*. Cambridge: Cambridge University Press.

Parker, Oliver (1995). *Othello* [Film]. Culver City, CA: Columbia Pictures Industries.

Pedersen, David Budtz (2016). 'Integrating Social Sciences and Humanities in Interdisciplinary Research', *Palgrave Communications*, 2: 1–7.

Percival, Brian (2005). *ShakespeaRe-Told: Much Ado about Nothing* [Film]. London: British Broadcasting.

Phipps, Alison (2021). 'White Tears, White Rage: Victimhood and (as) Violence in Mainstream Feminism', *European Journal of Cultural Studies*, 24(1): 81–93.

Pujante, Ángel-Luis & Keith Gregor (2023). 'Managerial Shakespeare and Troilus and Cressida', *Linguaculture*, 14(1): 83–100.

Rabkin, Norman (1977). 'Rabbits, Ducks, and Henry V', *Shakespeare Quarterly*, 28(3): 279–296.

Rackin, Phyllis (2005). *Shakespeare and Women*. Oxford: Oxford University Press.

Radford, Michael (2004). *The Merchant of Venice* [Film]. Beverly Hills, CA: Metro-Goldwyn-Mayer Studios.

Robinson, Simon (2016). 'Integrity and Its Counterfeits: Shakespeare's Henriad', *Palgrave Communications*, 2(1): 1–9.

Robinson, Cheska (2017). 'Add More STEAM to Your Classes', *Science Scope*, 41(1): 18–22.

Rogers, Jami (2022). *British Black and Asian Shakespeareans: Integrating Shakespeare, 1966–2018*. London: The Raden Shakespeare.

Ruiter, David (2020). *The Arden Research Handbook of Shakespeare and Social Justice*. London: The Arden Shakespeare.

Sarkar, Abhishek (2021). 'Teaching Shakespeare in Bengal: Tradition and Its Discontents'. Paper for 'Teaching Shakespeare' seminar, British Shakespeare Association – online conference.

Semler, Liam (2020). In 'Video Interview with Editors Gillian Woods and Liam E. Semler', website Cambridge Elements. Shakespeare and Pedagogy. www.cambridge.org/core/publications/elements/shakespeare-and-pedagogy. Last accessed 18 October 2024. www.youtube.com/watch?time_continue=119&v=rllMxDc_6Q4&embeds_referring_euri=https%3A%2F%2Fwww.cambridge.org%2Fcore%2Fpublications%2Felements%2Fshakespeare-and-pedagogy&source_ve_path=MzY4NDIsMjg2NjY&feature=emb_logo.

Semler, Liam E., Claire Hansen & Jacqueline Manuel, eds. (2023). *Reimagining Shakespeare Education: Teaching and Learning through Collaboration*. Cambridge: Cambridge University Press.

Smith, Emma, ed. (2021). *Shakespeare Survey 74: Shakespeare and Education*. Cambridge: Cambridge University Press.

Smith, Jeffrey K. & Lisa F. Smith (2019). 'Grading in Higher Education', in Thomas R. Guskey & Susan M. Brookhart, eds., *What We Know about Grading: What Works, What Doesn't, and What's Next*. Alexandria, VA: Association for Supervision & Curriculum Development, 195–213.

Stavreva, Kirilka (2022). 'Interview with Stephan Wolfert on Shakespeare, Trauma, and Mapping Affective Theatre Communities', *Cahiers Elisabéthains: A Journal of English Renaissance Studies*, 108(1): 78–90.

Stein, Mark (2005). 'The Othello Conundrum: The Inner Contagion of Leadership', *Organization Studies*, 26(9): 1405–1419.

Thompson, Ayanna, ed. (2021). *The Cambridge Companion to Shakespeare and Race*. Cambridge: Cambridge University Press.

Thompson, Ayanna & Laura Turchi (2016). *Teaching Shakespeare with Purpose: A Student-Centred Approach*. London: The Arden Shakespeare.

Thurman, Chris & Sandra Young (2023). *Global Shakespeare and Social Injustice: Towards a Transformative Encounter*. London: The Arden Shakespeare.

Tillman Jr., George (2018). *The Hate U Give* [Film]. Los Angeles, CA: 20th Century Fox.

Toohey, Peter (2004). *Melancholy, Love, and Time: Boundaries of the Self in Ancient Literature*. Ann Arbor, MI: University of Michigan Press.

Tosh, Will (2017). 'What You Will', online posted 11 May 2017. https://web.archive.org/web/20170605103925/https://blog.shakespearesglobe.com/post/160546033578/gender-in-twelfth-night. Last accessed on 18 October 2024.

Townsley, Matt (2022). *Using Grading to Support Student Learning*. New York: Routledge.

Turchi, Laura B. (2023). 'Shakespeare Pedagogy and Anti-Racist Curriculum Initiatives', in Pamela Bickley & Jenny Stevens, eds., *Shakespeare, Education and Pedagogy: Representations, Interactions and Adaptations*. London: Routledge, 145–153.

University of Groningen (2021). *Making Connections: 21/26. Strategic Plan University of Groningen*. Groningen: University of Groningen. www.rug.nl/about-ug/policy-and-strategy/strategic-plan/strategisch-plan-eng-2021.pdf. Last accessed on 18 October 2024.

University College Groningen (2023). *Curriculum Education University College Groningen*. www.rug.nl/ucg/education/. Last accessed on 18 October 2024.

Warner, Nicholas (2007). 'Screening Leadership through Shakespeare: Paradoxes of Leader-Follower Relations in *Henry V* on Film', *The Leadership Quarterly*, 18(1): 1–15.

Wekker, Gloria (2016). *White Innocence: Paradoxes of Colonialism and Race*. Durham, NC: Duke University Press.

Whedon, Joss (2012). *Much Ado about Nothing* [Film]. Los Angeles, CA: Bellwether Pictures.

Wilson, Jeffrey R. (2020). *Shakespeare and Trump*. Philadelphia, PA: Temple University Press.

Winston, Bruce E., & Patterson, Kathleen (2006). 'An Integrative Definition of Leadership', *International Journal of Leadership Studies*, 1(2): 6–66.

Yin, Robert K. (2018). *Case Study Research and Applications: Design and Methods*. Thousand Oaks, CA: Sage.

Cambridge Elements ≡

Shakespeare and Pedagogy

Liam E. Semler
The University of Sydney

Liam E. Semler is Professor of Early Modern Literature in the Department of English at the University of Sydney. He is author of Teaching Shakespeare and Marlowe: Learning versus the System (2013) and co-editor (with Kate Flaherty and Penny Gay) of Teaching Shakespeare beyond the Centre: Australasian Perspectives (2013). He is editor of Coriolanus: A Critical Reader (2021) and co-editor (with Claire Hansen and Jackie Manuel) of Reimagining Shakespeare Education: Teaching and Learning through Collaboration (Cambridge, forthcoming). His most recent book outside Shakespeare studies is The Early Modern Grotesque: English Sources and Documents 1500–1700 (2019). Liam leads the Better Strangers project which hosts the open-access Shakespeare Reloaded website (shakespearereloaded.edu.au).

Gillian Woods
University of Oxford

Gillian Woods is an Associate Professor and Tutorial Fellow in English at Magdalen College, University of Oxford. She is the author of *Shakespeare's Unreformed Fictions* (2013; joint winner of Shakespeare's Globe Book Award), *Romeo and Juliet: A Reader's Guide to Essential Criticism* (2012), and numerous articles about Renaissance drama. She is the co-editor (with Sarah Dustagheer) of *Stage Directions and Shakespearean Theatre* (2018). She is currently working on a new edition of *A Midsummer Night's Dream* for Cambridge University Press, as well as a Leverhulme-funded monograph about Renaissance Theatricalities. As founding director of the Shakespeare Teachers' Conversations, she runs a seminar series that brings together university academics, school teachers and educationalists from non-traditional sectors, and she regularly runs workshops for schools.

ADVISORY BOARD

Janelle Jenstad, *University of Victoria*

Farah Karim-Cooper, *Shakespeare's Globe*

Bi-qi Beatrice Lei, *National Taiwan University*

Florence March, *Université Paul-Valéry Montpellier*

Peggy O'Brien, *Folger Shakespeare Library*

Paul Prescott, *University of California Merced*

Abigail Rokison-Woodall, *University of Birmingham*

Emma Smith, *University of Oxford*

Patrick Spottiswoode, *Shakespeare's Globe*

Jenny Stevens, *English Association*

Ayanna Thompson, Arizona State University

Joe Winston, *University of Warwick*

About the Series

The teaching and learning of Shakespeare around the world is complex and changing. Elements in Shakespeare and Pedagogy synthesises theory and practice, including provocative, original pieces of research, as well as dynamic, practical engagements with learning contexts.

Cambridge Elements

Shakespeare and Pedagogy

Elements in the Series

Reading Shakespeare through Drama
Jane Coles and Maggie Pitfield

Podcasts and Feminist Shakespeare Pedagogy
Varsha Panjwani

Anti-Racist Shakespeare
Ambereen Dadabhoy and Nedda Mehdizadeh

Teaching Shakespeare and His Sisters: An Embodied Approach
Emma Whipday

Shakespeare and Place-Based Learning
Claire Hansen

Critical Pedagogy and Active Approaches to Teaching Shakespeare
Jennifer Kitchen

Teaching with Interactive Shakespeare Editions
Laura B. Turchi

Disavowing Authority in the Shakespeare Classroom
Huw Griffiths

The Pedagogy of Watching Shakespeare
Bethan Marshall, Myfanwy Edwards and Charlotte Dixie

Teaching English as a Second Language with Shakespeare
Fabio Ciambella

Shakespeare and Neurodiversity
Laura Seymour

Transdisciplinary Shakespeare Pedagogy
Coen Heijes

A full series listing is available at: www.cambridge.org/ESPG

For EU product safety concerns, contact us at Calle de José Abascal, 56–1°, 28003 Madrid, Spain or eugpsr@cambridge.org.

www.ingramcontent.com/pod-product-compliance
Ingram Content Group UK Ltd.
Pitfield, Milton Keynes, MK11 3LW, UK
UKHW022243220326
469255UK00019B/333